The Current Collegiate Hookup Culture

The Current Collegiate Hookup Culture

Dating Apps, Hookup Scripts, and Sexual Outcomes

Aditi Paul

LEXINGTON BOOKS

Lanham • Boulder • New York • London

Published by Lexington Books
An imprint of The Rowman & Littlefield Publishing Group, Inc.
4501 Forbes Boulevard, Suite 200, Lanham, Maryland 20706
www.rowman.com

86-90 Paul Street, London EC2A 4NE

British Library Cataloguing in Publication Information Available

Library of Congress Cataloging-in-Publication Data

Names: Paul, Aditi, author.
Title: The current collegiate hookup culture : dating apps, hookup scripts, and sexual
    outcomes / Aditi Paul.
Description: Lanham : Lexington Books, [2022] | Includes bibliographical references.
Identifiers: LCCN 2021051412 (print) | LCCN 2021051413 (ebook) |
    ISBN 9781793633606 (cloth ; alk. paper) | ISBN 9781793633613 (ebook)
Subjects: LCSH: College students—Sexual behavior—United States. | Dating (Social
    customs)—United States. | Online dating—United States. | Sexual ethics—United
    States. | College students—United States—Social life and customs
Classification: LCC HQ27 .P374 2022 (print) | LCC HQ27 (ebook) |
    DDC 306.70973—dc23/eng/20211022
LC record available at https://lccn.loc.gov/2021051412
LC ebook record available at https://lccn.loc.gov/2021051413

To my Guru, my all.

Contents

List of Tables

Acknowledgments

I would like to express my heartfelt gratitude to everyone who made this book turn from an idea into reality: first, my colleagues in the Department of Communication Studies at Pace University—Barry Morris, Mary Ann Murphy, Emilie Zaslow, Seong Jae Min, Melvin Williams, and Mary Stambaugh—thank you for your support. I would like to especially thank Marcella Szablewicz and Adam Klein for providing valuable feedback on my initial book proposal. Based on their feedback, I revised the proposal, which ultimately got accepted by Lexington Books.

Next, I want to thank Pace University for providing a research grant and scholarly release time that helped me bring this book to fruition. A huge shout out to Brynne Townley from Qualtrics, who helped me gather quality participant responses for the survey that informed the research presented in this book. Lucy Dolcich, my wonderful coauthor, and Pace alumna, thank you for cowriting the chapter on hookup scripts and for providing feedback on the other book chapters; you are wise beyond your years, and it has been an honor knowing you.

Most of all, thank you to the wonderful editorial team at Lexington Books, particularly Nicolette Amstutz and Sierra Apaliski for their unrelenting patience, kindness, and grace. Without you, this book would not have been possible. I appreciate you.

And finally, thank you to my wonderful family for their moral support—my mom Namita Paul, my dad Dipak Paul, my sister Atrayee Sett and her family. Above all, thank you to my Guru Lt. Smt. Kinkori Jogeshori Debi or my beloved Shibanidi for her selfless love and acceptance. I offer my thousand obeisances to you. Joy Guru.

Chapter 1

Hookups

An Integral Part of the
American College Experience

If you ask American undergraduate students to describe their "typical college experience," that list would include *attending classes, stressing about scheduling and financial aid, unaccounted hours of napping between classes, complaining about cafeteria food, pulling all-nighters*, and *negotiating grades with professors*. But, most of us will agree that no college experience would be complete without students mentioning the occurrence of hookups, that is, short-term sexual encounters without any promise of commitment.

Multiple studies have shown that more than half of college students have at least one hookup experience before graduating college (Garcia et al., 2012; Kuperberg & Padgett, 2015). Scholars have cited several reasons that make the college student population more likely to engage in hookups than others. The first reason is attributed to college students being emerging adults. Arnett (2004) explains emerging adulthood as a developmental period in our lives when exploring our identities in terms of love, work, and worldviews is of paramount importance. Being in this developmental phase makes college students more open and willing to participate in unconventional sexual and romantic experiences such as hookups.

Another popularly cited reason for college students' overwhelming participation in hookups is their need to conform to the norms of the omnipresent *hookup culture* in college campuses. Wade (2017) clarifies that hookup culture is the perception students hold that hooking up is the norm of college life—if one does not do hook up, one essentially is missing out or worse failing at the college experience. Thus, more than hooking up to expand their sexual repertoire, students may be hooking up to gain a sense of belonging in college.

The perception of hookups being a normative college experience comes from a combination of two factors: the skewed representation of college life in movies and the pluralistic ignorance about hookups among college students. Movies such as *American Pie* and *Neighbors* have notoriously promoted and glorified the image of college life being one that is marked with wild parties overflowing with alcohol where boys and girls engage in sexually charged interactions that ultimately lead them hooking up. These movies prime students into believing that this is the new normal they are stepping into when they enter college. Impressionable students, in their need to conform, look for such opportunities to hook up and enact the "regular college life" script promoted in these movies (Wasylkiw & Currie, 2012).

Apart from the effect of media, college students' engagement in hookups has been ascribed to pluralistic ignorance, the misconception among individuals who believe that their personal beliefs are not congruent with the beliefs held by everyone else in the group. But they conform to the beliefs of the group, even if they may not be comfortable with it (Allport, 1924, 1933). Scholars have shown that such pluralistic ignorance about hookups exists among college students (Lambert, Kahn, & Apple, 2003; Reiber & Garcia, 2010). College students systematically overestimate the sexual experiences of their peers thinking that their close friends and the general student population hook up more frequently, have more sexually permissive attitudes than them, when the reality is significantly different. Paul and Hayes (2002) asked 187 students to estimate the percentage of college students they thought had hooked up and report about their own hookups. Students believed that 85% of college students had hooked up at least once, when in reality only 70% of college students ever hooked up. This false assumption of "everyone is doing it so I should do it too" ultimately pressures college students to hook up even when they may not be comfortable doing so.

IS THE MORAL PANIC SURROUNDING HOOKUPS LEGITIMATE?

Any significant societal change invites a sense of moral panic among people. When hookups started becoming a popular coupling strategy among college students, scholars and popular media were quick to claim that hookups are a perversion of the traditional courtship process and that hookups are leading to the demise of dating. We were flooded with articles like *The Death of Dating: Hook-up Culture Is a Relational Crisis*, *The Demise of Dating*, and *Tinder and the Dawn of the Dating Apocalypse*. The basic premise of these articles was that the college hookup culture actively encourages students to seek out multiple sexual partners to have "meaningless" sex, without any expectation of relational commitment. This pursuit of sexual gratification with reckless abandon and the active avoidance or apathy toward relational commitment triggered the moral panic surrounding hookups. Consequently, hookups were demonized, and dating was heralded as the golden standard of coupling among college students. But a look into the origins of dating reveals that dating and hooking up may have more in common than we have been conditioned to believe.

DATING: NOT WHAT IT USED TO BE

American sociologist Willard Waller was the first person to study the concept of dating. In his article "The Rating and Dating Complex," Waller (1937) described dating as a "peculiar" form of coupling because it was not true courtship, but a dalliance relationship that was purely motivated by thrill seeking and amusement. So, how did college students *date*? Waller (1937) found that dating comprised of college students attending victrola dances and socials organized at fraternity houses where the sex ratio would be maintained at six boys to every girl. Based on the centrality of fraternity houses, Waller (1937) concluded that dating was almost exclusively the privilege of fraternity men and that non-fraternity men were practically excluded. Waller (1937) also mentioned that behaviors such as "petting" and "necking" were common in dating. He criticized these dalliance relationships for their exploitative nature where male college students exploited women for their bodies. In return, female college students exploited men for gifts and money. Waller (1937) labeled this as "gold-digging."

In sum, Waller (1937) drew a very pessimistic conclusion from his observations of dating behaviors among college students with his biggest gripe being how dating was leading to the decay of the traditional mores of courtship. He complained,

> According to the old morality a kiss means something, a declaration of love means something, a number of Sunday evening dates in succession means some-thing, and these meanings are enforced by the customary law, while under the new morality such things may mean nothing at all—that is, they may imply no commitment of the total personality whatsoever.

Waller's (1937) main concern was that dating was causing the death of true relationships because physical acts, which conventionally held some significance and meaning, were now being rendered meaningless by dating.

WHAT CHANGED ABOUT DATING?

This seminal analysis by Waller (1937) brought dating to the fore of academic scrutiny. Subsequent researchers, however, challenged his pessimistic view on multiple grounds. First, Waller (1937) had centered his theory on a relatively small part of the dating process. On further examination, scholars found that dating was a more complex process than just attending parties, necking, and thrill seeking; there was more nuance to it. For instance, Herman (1955) found that students engaged in different forms of dating: (a) random dating: completely playing the field (different person each date), (b) casual dating: partly playing the field (occasionally date the same person), and (c) steadily dating: often dating the same person. What Waller (1937) described speaks more to *random dating* where college men and women are motivated to date multiple people to check compatibility with them before going steady with a particular person.

Second, scholars found that students did not date purely out of the need for thrill seeking and other hedonistic pursuits. Burgess, Locke, and Thomes (1963) provided a more realistic version of students' dating motivations and practices. Instead of contending that dating is the antithesis of courtship, the authors suggested that dating is just a different type of association, one that is governed by its own set of distinctive norms. They also found that students dated to build friendly associations with people from the opposite sex. Lowrie (1951) expanded on Burgess et al.'s (1963) work by identifying other reasons students had for dating, including dating for partner selection, dating for anticipatory socialization, and dating for hedonistic pleasures. Partner selection meant that students dated with the goal of finding a marriage partner. Anticipatory socialization meant that students wanted to learn how to interact with the opposite sex, work on their personality and poise, and know what qualities they wanted or did not want in their partners. Lastly, hedonistic pleasures included having fun, petting, and necking (in colloquial terms what is *making out*), and to gain status and prestige among peers.

As is evident from Lowrie's (1951) results, which also echoed the results of contemporary studies on dating, students dated to forge potential romantic relationships. Thus, students looked at dating as a gateway to traditional courtship, which would eventually lead to marriage. Despite the overlap between dating and courtship, the fundamental difference between traditional courtship and dating can be summed up in one word: freedom. Dating provided students a degree of freedom that was not warranted by traditional courtship. Lowrie (1951) explained it well. He said, during colonial times and even during the early 1900s, when a boy courted a girl, it was assumed that the boy would invariably propose marriage to the girl. Dating transformed that expectation behind courtship, that is, the act of a man asking a woman out. Just because a man asks a woman out and that the two are seen in public together, once or repeatedly, that does not mean they are under any obligation to carry it through to marriage. "Dating participants have a minimum of accepted responsibility to continue the relationship," attested Lowrie (1951).

That dating was an end in itself without the demands of future involvement was a significant deviation from the previous cultural expectation of a man and a woman being obligated to marry just because they were romantically interested in each other.

Even though most of Waller's (1937) theory of dating was disproved or contradicted by subsequent researchers, one of his propositions was true—that true courtship can emerge from dating. In other words, even though the societal expectation of dating is that it is a standalone relationship with no expectation of formal commitment in the future, it can always lead to commitment. As a man and a woman discover their compatibility and continue dating, they may get more emotionally involved with each other. It is during this stage that Waller (1937) said, "the mores of dating break down and the behavior of the individuals is governed by the older mores of progressive commitment."

In sum, scholars concluded that dating was not a perversion of the traditional courtship process. Instead, dating served as a developmental stage in the courtship process which allowed individuals to figure out their compatibility with each other without any pressure of commitment.

In the same way, empirical evidence in hookup literature has also shown that hooking up is not causing the downfall of traditional courtship. Rather, hooking up serves as a step toward dating which then leads to a committed relationship. I expand on these studies on hookups and their findings in the next section.

DEFINING HOOKUPS

Just like Waller (1937) was confused when he examined dating, the then-novel form of coupling, scholars who set out to study hookups were equally baffled by the vagueness of the term *hookups*. This vagueness has led to a considerable amount of variation in the way this term has been defined in extant literature. When studying hookups among college students, most researchers have provided their own conceptual definition of the term while some have relied on students describing the term. Researchers who used student-led definitions of hookups justified that students' definition of the term would be more accurate in capturing the authentic nature of hookups, something that scholars, who are not active participants in the hookup culture, may have missed.

Paul, Manus, and Hayes (2000) were the first researchers to provide a formal definition of the term hookup in their study *"Hookups": Characteristics and correlates of college students' spontaneous and anonymous sexual experiences*. They defined hookup as "a sexual encounter, usually only lasting one night, between two people who are strangers or brief acquaintances. Some physical interaction is typical but may or may not include sexual intercourse" (p. 79). This definition implies that hookups are (a) a one-time event, (b) between two people who have little to no familiarity with each other, and (c) who may engage in a variety of sexual behaviors that may or may not involve oral, vaginal, or anal sex. Subsequent scholars have altered these three elements of the definition, vis-à-vis the frequency, level of familiarity with partner, and types of sexual behaviors in a hookup.

Hooking Up as a One-Time Event

Considering new empirical evidence, the first revision suggested to Paul et al.'s (2000) definition was to the phrase "usually only lasting one night." The implication of this phrase is that hookups are supposed to be a one-time sexual event. However, students frequently report hooking up with the same person more than once. England, Shafer, and Fogarty (2008) analyzed the hookup experiences of 2,510 students from 5 American universities and found that 50% of these students reported hooking up with their partners only once, while the rest of the 50% reported hooking up with their partners more than once, sometimes exceeding 10 times. Based on this finding, researchers have updated the definition of hookups to indicate that hookups can occur once or several times with the same person.

Hooking Up Only with Strangers

The second revision was done to the clause "strangers or brief acquaintances" when evidence started emerging that college students rarely hooked up with people they were not familiar with. For instance, a study examining the effect of partner familiarity on hookup behaviors showed that less than 8% of 828 college students had their most recent hookup with a stranger they had met that night. The majority reported hooking up with someone they already knew from before (Labrie et al., 2014). In fact, hookups were most likely to occur between friends. A survey of 1,468 undergraduates showed that 8.4% hooked up with a stranger, 24% hooked up with a casual acquaintance, 13.8% hooked up with an ex-boyfriend or girlfriend, and a whopping 52.8% reported hooking up with a friend (Fielder & Carey, 2010).

Based on the familiarity with hookup partners (friends vs. strangers/ acquaintances) and the number of times students hookup with their partners (one time vs. reoccurring), Claxton and Van Dulmen (2013) identified three types of hookup experiences: one-night stands, booty calls, and friends with benefits. One-night stands are the most closely aligned with Paul et al.'s (2000) definition because it implies two people who met each other for the first time in a social setting engaging in unplanned sexual activities with each other. Compared to this, booty calls occur between two individuals who are not friends but they hookup with each other multiple times, and this hookup usually occurs when one person gets in touch with the other late at night, possibly under the influence of alcohol. Lastly, friends with benefits are those hookups that occur between two individuals who are friends who regularly hookup with each other but have no romantic expectations from each other.

Irrespective of the variations of hookups that college students are engaging in, there is one common theme across all these variations of the definition of hookups—it is the idea of "no strings attached," the lack of commitment, absence of romantic intention, and complete emotional detachment from hookup partners. Garcia and Reiber (2008) summed it up by spelling out three rules that define hookups: (a) the individuals engaging in hookups are not in a traditional romantic relationship (i.e., boyfriend/girlfriend), (b) there are no prior discussions of what behaviors will occur during the hookup, and (c) there is no promise that the hookup will lead to any subsequent hookups or a romantic relationship.

Hooking Up Involving a Variety of Sexual Behaviors

Lastly, rather than revising the phrase "some physical interaction is typical" in Paul et al.'s (2000) definition, subsequent research studies identified specific types of sexual behaviors that students engage in during hookups. In studies that took the researcher-led approach to defining hookups, these specific sexual behaviors during a typical hookup were identified by providing study participants with a list of possible sexual behaviors and asking them to select all of the behaviors they engaged in during hookups (Lewis et al., 2015). According to the results, the commonly cited sexual behaviors during a typical hookup include kissing, touching of breasts and buttocks, genital stimulation, oral sex, vaginal sex, and anal sex. Students can engage in any combination of these behaviors during hookups.

For studies that adopted a student-led approach to defining hookups found similar results. Olmstead, Conrad, and Anders (2018) asked 253 freshmen to identify the types of behaviors they would expect to occur during hookups. Based on a content analyses of the open-ended responses provided by students, the researchers identified six variations of behaviors that college students expected to happen during hookups: (a) "sex" left undefined (any type of sexual contact), (b) making out (kissing, touching, fondling), (c) a range of sexual activities (multiple sexual behaviors without specifying any in particular), (d) "sex" defined as penetrative intercourse, (e) the "all but sex" continuum (inclusive of most sexual behaviors except for intercourse), and (f) hanging out or going on a date (non-sexual).

Thus, the vague and ambiguous nature of the term *hookup* allows a range of sexual activities to be included under this one umbrella term. Certain sexual behaviors from this range of sexual behaviors are more likely to occur than others. Most students report *making out* during hookups. These types of hookups consist of non-penetrative sexual acts such as kissing and touching of breasts and genitalia. According to Fielder and Carey's (2010) results, kissing, sexual touching, and oral sex were the most common sexual behaviors during hookups; less than half of the students reported engaging in vaginal sex, and a very small percentage of students reported having anal sex during hookups. The discrepancy between more college students reporting hooking up and less college students reporting having sex can be because most college students may be just *making out* rather than having sex. Another factor that can explain this discrepancy is that most college students do not consider oral sex as "sex." As one male college student in England et al.'s (2008) study commented, "There's a *big* line between oral sex and intercourse." This means that all the instances that students reported engaging in oral sex are not considered as intercourse. This suggests that students' understanding of what sex is includes only vaginal and anal sex.

Since Paul et al.'s (2000) seminal study, a number of scholars have examined the hookup phenomenon within the American college context. The extant literature on hookups can be broadly categorized into three themes: (a) studies that have examined demographic and psychological factors that affect students' participation in hookups, (b) the type of actions (i.e., scripts) that students follow during hookups, and (c) the physical and emotional consequences of hookups. I provide an overview of the three themes in the section below and expand on each of these themes in subsequent chapters.

What Factors Affect Hookups?

The first dominant theme in hookup literature is examining factors that predict hookups. Researchers from fields such as communication, psychology, and sociology have conducted numerous studies to answer the question— *which students are more likely to hook up?*

The most frequently studied factor has been gender. Scholars have argued that male college students are more likely to hook up, have a greater number of hookup partners, and engage in higher-order sexual hookup behaviors compared to female college students. They have cited evolutionary, psychological, and sociological reasons to buttress their claim (England & Thomas, 2006; Grello, Welsch, & Harper, 2006). First, men are biologically wired to prefer short-term sexual partners and maximize the number of sexual partners for genetic success. Second, men have more liberal views on sex compared to women. Third, societal double standards reward males and punish females for sexual exploration.

Alongside gender, student's sexual orientation has also been shown to affect their participation in the college hookup culture. Scholars have criticized the lack of research on LGBTQIA+ groups because most of the research on college hookups has been focused on heterosexual students. A part of this has been attributed to (a) the underrepresentation of LGBTQIA+ students as a majority of the college student population being heterosexual, and (b) the heterosexual bias in the instruments used to measure sexual behaviors of college students (Watson, Snapp, & Wang, 2017). The limited research available on sexual minority students have yielded mixed results with some studies concluding that heterosexual students will be more likely to hook up compared to sexual minorities, and some studies refuting these results (Barrios & Lundquist, 2012; Eisenberg, 2001).

College students' racial and ethnic identity has also been shown to affect their participation in the hookup culture. However, similar to research on sexual orientation, results from these studies have been contradictory and inconclusive. Some studies have shown that Black students have more permissive attitudes toward sex and report having more casual sexual encounters compared to White students. On the contrary, other studies have found that a greater number of White students reported hooking up at least once in the previous year. A common finding between these studies was the lower ranking of Asian students compared to other racial groups. While some scholars have argued that certain racial groups' students are more sexually permissive, hence more likely to hook up, others have insisted that the low number of hookups among racial minorities may have less to do with their sexual conservativeness and more to do with their need to avoid being tokenized or stereotyped (Kuperberg & Padgett, 2016; McClintock, 2010).

Scholars have also examined the effect that students' religious beliefs have on their sexual decision-making process (Brimeyer & Smith, 2012; Regnerus, 2007). Since most religions promote sexual abstinence, scholars have expected that students who are religious would be less likely to hook up compared to students who are not religious. Some studies have found this claim to be true, that is, students who are more devout report lower number of sexual partners, while others have failed to establish such a connection. Some studies have also shown a reverse effect of religious membership on hookups where students from religious colleges hook up more compared to students from non-denominational institutions.

Besides students' gender, sexual orientation, race, and religion, scholars have also cited students' group memberships and their educational aspirations as factors that affect students' hookup behaviors (Adkins et al.,

2015; Mosley, 2009; Owen et al., 2010). Students belonging to Greek life (fraternities and sororities) have consistently been shown to have a greater likelihood of hooking up compared to their non-Greek counterparts. Similar trends have been shown for students who belong to athletic teams as well. Since hookups are essentially viewed as a recreational activity, students who place a high premium on their educational career (i.e., who maintain a high GPA and aspire for advanced degrees) will be less likely to spend their time hooking up and more likely to devote that time in studying. On the flipside, these students may be more likely to pursue short-term sexual relationships instead of investing their time in long-term relationships. As with other factors, research examining the association between academic performance and hookup behaviors has yielded inconsistent results.

Lastly, in terms of psychological and behavioral factors, students' attitude toward sex and their past sexual behaviors have been shown to predict their engagement in or abstention from hookups. In particular, students who have more permissive attitudes toward sex and have had previous sexual experience will be more likely to hook up and have more hookup partners compared to sexually conservative and inexperienced students (Katz & Schneider, 2013; Olmstead et al., 2013; Townsend & Wasserman, 2011). Unlike demographic factors, studies examining the relationship between sexual permissiveness and previous sexual experience have yielded consistent results.

What Happens during Hookups?

The second dominant theme in extant hookup literature is examining hookup scripts, the sequence of actions students follow during a hookup. The cultural hookup script—the hookup script perpetrated by movies and television—involves going to parties, usually hosted in fraternity parties, getting drunk, and hooking up with strangers in an inebriated state. Survey analyses and script analyses of students' interpersonal hookup scripts—how they actually hook up—have shown that they both follow and deviate from the cultural hookup script. Studies examining students' interpersonal hookup scripts have found that drinking alcohol was a dominant element of the hookup script (Kuperberg & Padgett, 2015). Consistent with the cultural understanding of hookups, these studies have also found that hookups involve some sort of physical contact ranging from kissing to intercourse (Eaton et al., 2016). Empirical evidence also suggests that students do not meet their hookup partners only in party settings; students report hooking up with individuals they had met in school or even at work (Kuperberg & Padgett, 2015). However, most of the studies that have analyzed hookup scripts seem to have an implicit assumption that hookups are solely initiated at parties. To my knowledge, there is no study that has examined if and how the hookup scripts differ based on the location where students meet their hookup partners.

What Are the Consequences of Hooking Up?

The third most dominant theme in extant hookup literature is examining the outcomes of engaging in hookups. The "no strings attached" laissez-faire nature of hookups has concerned academics because of the potential negative physical and psychological consequences it can have on students, especially female college students. Empirical research has confirmed their concerns as hookups have been associated with heightened risk of contracting sexually transmitted infections (STIs), occurrences of sexual assault, and feelings of depression and regret. Furthermore, college women have also been shown to experience less sexual satisfaction from hookup sex compared to sex that happens within the context of romantic relationships (Downing-Matibag & Geisinger, 2009; Fielder & Carey, 2010; Lambert, Kahn, & Apple, 2003).

A disproportionate amount of attention has been given to the negative consequences of hooking up. With emerging empirical evidence, scholars acknowledged that hookups can also have positive consequences. Studies have shown that students experience both positive and negative emotions after hooking up (England et al., 2008; Owen & Fincham, 2011; Snapp, Ryu, & Kerr, 2015). Some of these positive emotions are feelings of happiness, enjoyment of sexual activities, and also feeling good about their own bodies. However, consistent with the gender gap in sexual behaviors, scholars have claimed that college men would be more likely to report positive feelings post hooking up compared to college women.

WHAT IS MISSING IN EXTANT LITERATURE?

In the article titled *Hook-up Culture: Setting a New Research Agenda,* Heldman and Wade (2010) suggested that environmental and societal factors such as co-ed dorms and sexualization of content in media contribute to the formation of a space conducive for hookups. These factors increase the opportunities for men and women to interact freely and cohabitate with each other, which may then lead them engaging in sexual activities with each other. One such societal force that fueled the already rampant hookup culture in college campuses was the use of dating applications (app) such as *Tinder* to find hookup partners.

The Lure of Dating Apps among College Students

Before discussing the role of dating apps in the hookup culture, it is important to acknowledge the general popularity of dating apps among college students.

According to Pew Research, 48% of 18- to 24-year-olds reported using dating apps in 2020, compared to 22% in 2015 and 5% in 2013. This exponential rise in popularity of dating apps among college-aged students has been ascribed to five factors: mobility, authenticity, proximity, visual dominance, and immediacy.

First, unlike online dating website sites, dating apps like *Tinder* works on a mobile phone. People no longer have to take the extra step of logging into their computers to access their online dating profiles; it is now readily available to them in the palm of their hands. Second, dating app users do not have to create their online dating profiles and populate it with a ton of biographical information. Instead, they can now set up their dating profiles by linking their preexisting social media profiles like *Facebook* to their dating apps, composing a short "bio" section, and uploading a few of their pictures. The use of social media profiles as a basis for dating profiles affords a degree of authenticity and validity as it anchors their identities to other public platforms.

After curating their dating profiles, users can choose the radius within which they want to find potential partners. This ensures that the app only shows potential matches who are currently near them. Apart from distance, users can also utilize other filters such as age, race, religion, and other preferences to screen partners. Following this, dating apps populate users' screens with choices of potential partners. The apps maximize the visual element usage by displaying the profile pictures of the potential partners in a way that take up the whole phone screen. If users are attracted to the individuals displayed on their screens, they can swipe right on their screen to show interest or swipe left on their screen to reject. If a mutual selection occurs, that is, both users swiped right on each other, users can then proceed to have an online chat with each other and eventually may even decide to meet face to face.

This fast-paced matchmaking and convenient way of meeting compatible partners attracted college students to use such apps. Jordan Crook, the CEO of Tech Crunch, also argued that the game-like design of Tinder is another reason that lures people to keep using the app. In his article *Hate It Or Love It, Tinder's Right Swipe Limit Is Working,* Crook explained,

> Users want to swipe more because that is the game of Tinder, but the match is the equivalent of a turbocharged Like on another social network. It's not just a friend giving you a hat-tip on your photo or some random follower favoriting your tweet. It's someone who might actually like you, someone who may potentially want to have sex with you. The stakes are raised, and so is the reward.

Dating Apps as Venues to Meet Hookup Partners

Two unique affordances of dating apps that made them a viable choice for college students particular to meet hookup partners are (a) a large partner pool and (b) a relative anonymity. First, dating apps provide students with access to a larger pool of potential sexual partners to choose from, one that is beyond the confines of a traditional college setting. In 2018, the dating app *Tinder* even launched a service called *Tinder U* that allowed students to connect with other students with greater ease. Second, the relative anonymity warranted by dating apps alleviates the stigma associated with initiating hookups in person. This stigma can be felt by certain demographics such as females and LGBTQIA+ community who are often penalized for their sexuality.

The unprecedented popularity of dating apps among college-aged people piqued the interest of academics from various fields. Griffin, Canevello, and McAnulty (2018) surveyed 409 heterosexual college students and found that 39% of college students used dating apps. Among them, 31% used *Tinder* to have fun, 11% used *Tinder* to meet new people, and 4% used *Tinder* for hookups. Similar trends have been found in other studies examining dating app use among American college students (Lefebvre, 2018). As evidenced in these studies, despite the popularity of *Tinder*, it is rarely used as a *hookup app*, that is, using the app with the sole purpose of finding hookup partners. However, there is no denying that dating apps like *Tinder* have added another potential venue for students to meet hookup partners. As one student in Lefebvre's (2018) explained,

> I like to connect with people and I like to have sex. Those are the two primary motivations that I have for using any dating application. I chose to try Tinder because I knew a couple of people who had some success with it. It also seemed like a simple enough process, and I knew it was popular and wanted to find out why for myself.

Before the introduction of Tinder, the conventional means for college students to meet hookup partners was through parties, through institutional contexts such as class, student clubs, and dorms, through common friends, and through other affiliations such as church and the workplace. Today, these percentages may have changed owing to the introduction of dating apps as a context for meeting hookup partners. Despite this significant change in college life milieu, little to no research has examined if and how hookups that ensue from meeting partners through dating apps differ from hookups that ensue from meeting partners through conventional means like parties and school.

To my knowledge, Kuperberg and Padgett (2015) are the only researchers that have accounted for the effect of meeting contexts on students' dating and hookup behaviors. They analyzed the data from Online College Social Life Survey (OCSLS) that included 13,976 dates and 12,068 hookup encounters reported by students between 2005 and 2011 from 22 American colleges. When analyzing the effect of meeting context of partners, the researchers examined online meeting contexts as a combination of social networking sites, personal ads, and dating sites such as "adultfriendfinder.com." Their results showed that only 2.5% of students reported hooking up with someone they had met their partners online. This low percentage can be attributed to the timeline of data collection—the data collection stopped in 2011, around the time online dating apps like *Tinder* were gaining prominence in college campuses. Thus, Kuperberg and Padgett's (2015) study, despite its representative and large college student sample, failed to capture the current hookup scenarios in American college campuses.

THE PURPOSE OF THIS BOOK

My main goal in this book is to provide an accurate picture of the contemporary hookup culture in American college campuses. To accomplish this goal, I include dating apps as a venue for college students to meet hookup partners, along with other conventional meeting contexts such as parties, school, and work. I examine if and how dating app–initiated hookups differ from hookups initiated through other meeting contexts in three ways:

- First, I identify the demographic and psychological variables that distinguish students who tend to meet their hookup partners through dating apps versus conventional contexts such as parties, school, and work.
- Second, I examine the differences in scripts students use when hooking up with partners met through dating apps versus parties, school, or work.
- Third, I compare the positive and negative physical and emotional outcomes experienced by students when hooking up with partners met through dating apps versus parties, school, or work.

Together with assessing the effect of meeting contexts, I also account for the impact that gender has on hookups as previous research has repeatedly shown that hookup experiences of college women vary significantly from hookup experiences of college men.

Beyond accounting for the role of dating apps in the contemporary hookup culture, I also discuss the role of sexually permissive practices like sugar dating that are progressively gaining traction among college students. I discuss how sugar dating sites such as *Seeking Arrangement* and *Whats Your Price* are providing a context beyond hookups for students to experiment with

casual sex. I identify factors that make some students more willing to participate in sugar dating compared to others. Furthermore, I examine if and how
participation in sugar dating is related to students' regular hookup behaviors.
Finally, I conclude my discussion on the contemporary hookup culture by
calling to attention the exclusion of international students' unique hookup
experiences, and how this exclusion of a significant faction of the student
body can challenge the generalizability of extant scholarship on hookups.

Data Collection

I recruited Qualtrics to conduct the data collection for this study who administered the survey to a nationally representative sample of US-based college
students. Students needed to meet two criteria to be included in the final
sample for this study.

1. Students needed to be currently enrolled in an educational institute in the
   United States (could be private, public, four-year, university, liberal arts
   colleges or community colleges).
2. Students needed to have at least one hookup experience in their lives.
   They were presented with this prompt at the beginning of the survey:

   *A hookup is a sexual encounter, usually lasting only one night, between
   two people who are strangers or brief acquaintances. Some physical interaction is typical but may or may not include sexual intercourse (vaginal
   or anal).*

   *Examples of physical interaction include kissing or making out, breast
   stimulation, genital stimulation, and oral sex.*

Following this prompt, they were asked to indicate the estimated number
of people they had hooked up with in their lives. Students who reported having zero partners were excluded from the study. The final sample size for
this study consisted of 318 college students. The survey included a series
of questions pertaining to their sociodemographic information, details about
their most recent hookup experience, their sexual attitudes, and their sexual
history. On average, the survey took 19.20 minutes to complete.

To summarize, this book adds to the rich body of literature that explores
the hookup culture dominant in American college campuses. I hope the
research presented in this book helps us rethink our assumptions to gain an
understanding that more accurately represents how present-day college students engage in hookups. I begin this conversation by reviewing the sociodemographic and psychological factors that have often been associated with the
hookup behaviors of college students.

Chapter 2

Examining Sociodemographic and Psychological Correlates of College Student Hookups

Many assume that young adults who attend college in the United States will hook up at least once before they graduate. Multiple research studies have corroborated this assumption of hookups being a normative experience for American college students. A 2012 meta-analysis of the literature on college hookups showed that as many as 60%–80% of students reported some sort of hookup experience during their tenure in college (Garcia et al., 2012). Subsequent studies on college students have garnered similar results. Kuperberg and Padgett (2015) found around 62% of 22,454 students had hooked up since they started college. Not only do a majority of students' hookup, but they also accrue multiple hookup partners during their college years. Garneau et al.'s (2013) analysis showed that 77% of 562 college students reported hooking up with two or more individuals in the past 12 months.

A large fraction of research examining the hookup culture in American colleges has focused on identifying factors that determine college students' participation in or abstention from hookups. In this chapter, I provide an overview of the commonly cited sociodemographic and psychological factors that have been associated with college students' hookup behaviors. Following this, I analyze the data from my student sample to gauge in what ways their behaviors converge or diverge from extant research.

GENDER

Gender has been the most studied factor to predict students' hookup behaviors. Scholars have argued that male college students have a greater propensity for hooking up compared to female college students. This argument has been undergirded by either the sexual strategies theory or the sexual double standards theory.

According to sexual strategies theory (Buss & Schmidt, 1993), men and women have different mating strategies. This means that men and women have different parameters for selecting their sexual partners to ensure the successful transference of their genes. Women's reproduction ability is time-bound in that they only have a limited number of years between menstruation and menopause when they can birth children. Because of this time constraint, women are motivated to choose only those sexual partners with whom they can produce healthy children. Women also look to ensure that their sexual partners have the necessary resources to provide for their children. For this reason, women are said to have a long-term relational orientation toward mating. Men, with no such reproductive constraints, ensure their genetic success by maximizing the number of female partners hoping that each partnership would lead to the creation of their progeny. Consequently, men prioritize short-term mating strategy. Even when men are in long-term relationships, this evolutionary programming makes them more accepting of extradyadic sexual relations. Researchers who have found empirical evidence of male college students having more hookup partners compared to female college students have often used sexual strategies theory to rationalize their findings.

There is another school of thought in the academic community that explains the gender disparity in college students' hookup behaviors through the lens of the sexual double standard in society instead of sexual strategies theory (Buss & Schmidt, 1993). The term *sexual double standard* was first coined in 1956 by Ira Reiss in the article *The Double Standard in Premarital Sexual Intercourse: A Neglected Concept*. Reiss (1956) defined sexual double standard as judging men and women differently for engaging in premarital sex; society considered it unacceptable for women to engage in premarital sex but found it acceptable for men. Although the 1960s sexual revolution moved the needle toward a more gender egalitarian society, this sexual double standard is still present, albeit in a less pronounced way than before.

The presence of this sexual double standard is particularly palpable in the college hookup space. England and Thomas (2006), through their in-depth interviews of 270 heterosexual college students, found that men gain status when they hook up with a lot of women. However, if women hookup too much or have sex too easily, they earn a bad reputation. During these interviews, England and Thomas (2006) also asked participants if they thought the person they had hooked up with respected them less because of the hookup. 51% of women said yes compared to only 25% of men. This social stigma associated with hooking up discourages college women from hooking up as frequently as college men. A 20-year-old female student studying in a southern university summed up this sexual double standard in her testimony,

Girls get labeled if you hook up with too many people or you just hook up with a random person like the first night you meet 'em. They get labeled a slut. . . . And obviously you don't want that reputation of guys thinking they can just get in your pants whenever. (Currier, 2013)

The negative evaluation that college women receive for hooking up is not just from men, but they are harshly criticized by other women too. Milhausen and Herald (1999) asked 165 women at a Canadian university to describe either a man or a woman who had many sexual partners. Participants described the man as a *sexual predator* and a *player*. When describing the woman, they used words such as *slut, dirty, sleazy*, and *easy*. These results show that the female participants negatively evaluated both the man and the woman. But as the college students in England and Thomas's (2006) study insisted, even when men get a bad reputation for hooking up, it does not last long. Furthermore, as many as 46% of the female participants in Milhausen and Herald's (1999) study believed women themselves passed the harshest judgments toward other women's sexual behaviors. In comparison, only 12% of the women believed that men were the harsher judges. This shows that women uphold and perpetuate this sexual double standard despite being disadvantaged by it.

Over the years, college women have adopted certain coping mechanisms to avoid being stigmatized for their hookup behaviors. One of the commonly used strategies is leveraging the vagueness of the term *hookup* to veil their sexual activities. Currier (2013) found that college women strategically and intentionally used the term *hooked up* when they did not want to disclose higher-level sexual activities they may have participated in. Brianna, a 22-year-old White female participant, explained,

When people say, "We hooked up," you don't really know what they mean by that. They could be having sex every night. And you're assuming that they probably just made out or something like that.

Another strategy women have adopted to avoid being socially stigmatized for their hookup behaviors is by suppressing their sexual agency and their participation in higher-order sexual activities when reporting their hookups. England and Bearak (2014) analyzed the responses of 6,424 college students and found that 62% of college women reported their male partners initiating more of the sexual activities compared to only 39% of college men reported that their female partners initiated more of the sexual activities. In addition, 33% of college women compared to 40% of college men reported having vaginal intercourse during their most recent hookup.

In sum, proponents of both sexual strategies theory and sexual double standards are convinced that college men are more willing to engage in hookups and more likely to have multiple hookup partners compared to college women.

SEXUAL ORIENTATION

Research examining the effect of sexual orientation on students' hookup behaviors is limited in scope. Watson and associates (2017) reviewed the extant literature on college hookups, and concluded that research on lesbian, gay, and bisexual (LGB) youth was largely absent; heterosexual students have been the sole focus of most of these studies. The acute heteronormative nature of past literature can be attributed to the overrepresentation of heterosexual students in college campuses. The absence of LGB youth's sexual practices is ironic when one considers the pivotal role the LGB community played in the genesis of the hookup culture. Wade (2017) reminds us about this,

> If the young people living it up in cities in the 1920s are the hookup generation's ideological grandparents, the gay men of the 1970s might be their two dads. Gay men arguably invented the lifestyle; we may be seeing it in colleges today because young students on residential campuses are situated similarly to those who fled to gay enclaves during the height of gay liberation. (p. 115)

What Wade (2017) suggests here is that LGB youth, especially homosexual men, engaged in sexual relations with multiple partners as a way to express their sexual freedom and sexuality during the 1960s sexual revolution. This eventually led to the normalization of casual sex and the popularization of hookups. Thus, for LGB youth to be underrepresented and even erased from the current hookup narrative is unfortunate and problematic.

Comparing Heterosexual and LGB College Students' Hookup Participation

Within the narrow body of literature on lesbian, gay, and bisexual (LGB) college students, it has been contended that LGB students will be more likely to engage in sexual activities compared to their heterosexual counterparts. The greater tendency of LGB students to hookup has been ascribed to their need to explore their sexual identities and increase their sexual experience during college years.

Multiple studies have found support for these claims. Barrios and Lundquist (2012) compared sexual behaviors of 5,889 heterosexual and 330 male homosexual college students. Findings showed that heterosexual males reported having 3.37 sexual partners compared to 4.63 reported by homosexual males. Eisenberg (2001) analyzed the sexual behaviors of 8,658 undergraduate students and found that both bisexual male and female college students were more likely to report multiple sex partners compared to their heterosexual counterparts.

Over the years, prejudice toward sexual minorities has progressively declined. According to the 2020 World Values Survey, over 73% Americans have a medium to high acceptance of homosexuality. Schools and universities have also made significant strides to ensure the inclusion and safety of LGB youth. Online tools such as The Campus Pride Index, which rank orders universities based on their ability to ensure safety and inclusion of LGB students, also keep authorities in check. Despite these advances, LGB students have still reported facing discrimination, especially in the hookup culture that has been criticized for favoring White heterosexual men (Mays & Cochran, 2001). LGB students may also find it challenging to meet sexually compatible partners in predominantly heterosexual campuses. The fear of stigmatization and the lack of sexual partners may result in LGB students having fewer hookup partners compared to heterosexual students. This hypothesis is yet to be tested and supported.

RACE

Similar to sexual orientation, research examining the effect of students' racial identity on their hookup behaviors has also been sparse. The limited number of studies that have investigated this association have garnered contradictory results. There are two schools of thought on this matter. The first school believes that racial minority students in predominantly White campuses will be less likely to hook up compared to White students. The second school refutes this assertion and claims that racial minority students are just as likely to hook up as their White counterparts. Scholars who contend that racial minority students will have a lower hookup rate than White students attribute this racial difference to (a) lack of racial homophily and (b) avoidance of racial stereotypes.

Racial homophily, the preference of same-race partners, is an important factor in both sexual and romantic relationships. The fact that most college campuses in the United States are predominantly White impedes the chances of racial minority students to find partners to hook up with who belong to the same race. One of the first studies to examine this phenomenon was conducted by McClintock (2010). In her seminal study titled *When Does Race Matter? Race, Sex, and Dating at an Elite University*, the researcher examined patterns of racial homophily among 732 college students enrolled in Stanford University. She found that Black students were particularly isolated because they hardly had any interracial ties and limited their contact with Black communities. Thus, the paucity of same-race partners impedes the chances of hooking up for racial minority students.

In situations where racial minority students do meet compatible same-race partners, they are more motivated to turn that connection into a long-term relationship instead of squandering it on a short-term hookup. Eaton and her colleagues (2016) found that a larger percentage of Hispanic students compared to White students chose to go on a date with their partners instead of hooking up with them. Ray and Rosow (2010) also found similar results from interviewing 30 White and Black students belonging to fraternities. Results showed that Black males took romantic approaches while White males took sexual approaches toward women. When describing the advantages of being in a relationship, a Black male student shared,

> I'd say you get the companionship, the love. You've got somebody there in daytime hours, not just in nighttime hours. The nine to five hours they're going to be there to go out with you. They might send you out with some stuff, take you out to eat, go see a movie, and like it's that constant companionship.

In contrast, a White male student stated,

> Lots of sex. You can have it everyday without having to go out and get it. It's a lot easier, but you do have to put up with shit occasionally.

Another reason why scholars believe racial minority students are less likely to hookup is to avoid being stereotyped. Racial minority students may worry that if they engage in hookups more frequently, they will end up aligning themselves with media tropes that show Black and Latino women as promiscuous and fetishize Black men. Kuperberg and Padgett (2016) argued that the behaviors of college students who belong to a "visible minority group" (constitute less than 15% of the total population) can be extrapolated to the entire community they represent. This means that if Black students in a predominantly White campus hook up more frequently, then their behavior may be seen as a representation of the entire Black community. Thus, racial minority students may be motivated to either abstain from hookups or control their rate of hooking up to avoid such stereotyping.

Unlike Latinx and Black students, Asian students are subjected to a different sexual stereotype. Asians, especially Asian males, are thought to be sexually repressed, rigid, or inept. Media representations of the likes of the socially awkward Raj who cannot speak with women unless inebriated in the sitcom *Big Bang Theory* have perpetuated this stereotype. College students end up internalizing these stereotypes. As one of the participants in Chen's (2014) study on racialized hookups confessed, "I've heard that Asians—the entire Asian population: Indians and Southeast Asians and East Asians—have small dicks." Since sexual stereotypes affect the desirability of sexual partners, these negative tropes surrounding Asians hurt their chances of finding partners to hook up with in college.

Some scholars have found support for the claim that there is a racial difference in hookups, while others have found evidence contrary to this stance. For instance, Owen and a team of researchers (2010) found that 60.2% of White students reporting hooking up compared to only 42.4% of Hispanic students. Spell's (2017) analysis of 18.347 heterosexual college students' hookup behaviors showed that the White students had an average of 4.7 hookup partners. Compared to this, Latino and Black students reported an average of 3.1 students, and Asian students had an average of 2.2 hookup partners.

However, another group of studies have garnered results that are in sharp contrast to the ones above. Helm et al. (2015) surveyed 766 graduate and undergraduate students about their hookup behaviors and found that 52.2% of Latino students reported hooking up at least once in their lifetime. In comparison, 47.2% of Black students, 29.3% of White students, and only 20.3% of Asian/Pacific Islander students had hooked up at least once in their lifetime. Kuperberg and Padgett's (2015) results were similar in that Asian students were 2.5 times less likely to hook up than White students.

Before we consider these results as evidence of Asian students' reservation against hooking up, we should acknowledge two other findings from these studies. First, despite the lack of actual hookup behavior, Asian students, both male and female, were 55% more likely to desire more opportunities for hookups than their White counterparts. Furthermore, Helm et al. (2015) found that when Asian students did engage in hookups, they resorted to higher-order sexual behaviors such as sexual intercourse. This means that among the students who hooked up, Asian Americans had a greater likelihood of engaging in vaginal sex compared to lower-order sexual behaviors such as kissing, genital stimulation, and oral sex. These results show that the lower engagement in hookups among Asian students may not be because of their sexual reservation. Rather, it may be because there are not enough same-race students to select from. It could also be that Asian students are not considered as desirable sexual partners by other races because of the negative stereotypes perpetuated by media that color Asians are asexual or sexually incompetent.

RELIGION

Now the works of the flesh are evident: sexual immorality, impurity, sensuality, idolatry, sorcery, enmity, strife, jealousy, fits of anger, rivalries, dissensions, divisions, envy, drunkenness, orgies, and things like these. I warn you, as I warned you before, that those who do such things will not inherit the kingdom of God.

Galatians 5:19–21

A common denominator of all religions—Christianity, Judaism, Hinduism, Islam, and Buddhism—is their proscription from sexual promiscuity. The religious view on sexual relations is that they should occur within the context of matrimony. In other words, a man and woman should get married, and only then should they have sex with each other. Christianity goes so far as condemning sexually deviant behaviors such as "orgies," "sexual immorality," and "drunkenness," along with prohibiting premarital sex.

These sexual relations–related religious doctrines have found their way into educational institutes owing to government-mandated policies and programs. In the United States, 20 of the 29 states require that their sex education programs stress on abstinence until marriage. In 2018, President Trump proposed $277 million in new funding for abstinence-only programs. The efficacy of these programs in reducing teenage pregnancy and other risky sexual behaviors among adolescents and emerging adults has largely been questioned, but they continue to exist owing to governmental support. College environments are admittedly more secular and less government regulated than schools. But colleges also house campus ministries that promote similar principles of sexual abstention to its student members.

Based on this assumption, scholars have argued that religious college students will be less likely to hook up compared to non-religious college students. Regnerus (2007) conducted one of the most rigorous studies exploring the effect of religion on young Americans' sexuality. He examined four large data sets (National Survey of Youth and Religion, National Longitudinal Study of Adolescent Health [Add Health], National Youth Risk Behavior Survey, and 2002 National Survey of Family Growth) and presented his findings in the book titled *Forbidden Fruit: Sex & Religion in the Lives of American Teenagers.* One of his findings was that it was students' religious commitment, not their religious affiliation, that significantly affected their sexual behaviors and attitudes. A measure that has commonly been used as a proxy for religious commitment is how frequently students attend religious events. Multiple researchers have corroborated Regnerus's (2009) claim. Burdette et al. (2009) frequent church attendance reduced the odds of hooking up among a sample of 919 college-attending women. Brimeyer and Smith (2012) conducted a similar study on a sample consisting of both male and female students and found the same results, that is, church attendance was inversely related to the number of hookups.

There are three reasons why religious attendance has a dampening effect on students' propensity to hook up. First, the more students attend religious services, the more they are exposed to religious sermons that extol sexual purity. This repeated exposure reinforces students' belief in the importance of chastity and the ideal of *waiting until marriage*. Second, frequent attendance to religious events means that students have less time to engage in non-religious events. By extension, the chances of students being present in social situations such as parties which may present them with hookup opportunities are drastically curtailed. Third, students may fear that if they hook up, the news may spread within their religious network. This fear of earning a negative reputation and the possibility of being ostracized by their religious network can keep students from hooking up.

Interestingly, some researchers have found that attending religious gatherings more frequently had a reverse effect on sexual abstention. Kuperberg and Padgett (2016) in their analysis of hookup behaviors of 22,454 students found that college students who attended religious services had a higher rate of hooking up compared to students who did not attend religious services. Kuperberg and Padgett (2016) rationalized this counterintuitive result by arguing that students who go to religious services more often have a "strong social network to draw from when searching for potential partners" (p. 1091). This result can be interpreted in three ways. First, religious students are seeking sexual gratification despite the risk of damaging their reputation within the religious network. Second, religious students may be engaging in lower-order sexual behaviors such as kissing and genital touching and refraining from penetrative sex. This way, they do not violate the religious doctrines that advocate refraining from sex before marriage. Finally, religious students may be engaging in hooking up with the hope of turning the sexual companionship into a committed marital relationship. As a matter of fact, Kuperberg and Padgett (2015) found that students who attended religious services regularly had a higher rate of dating and partnering aside from hooking up compared to those who did not attend religious services at all. Thus, these religious students may be engaging in sexual relations with their partners hoping that it will eventuate in a committed relationship.

GREEK LIFE AND VARSITY

Fraternities and Sororities

Wade (2017), in her book *American Hookup: The New Culture of Sex on Campus,* said, "Hookup culture has descended upon college campuses like a fog. It's thickest on Greek Row, where students hope to find wild parties, hot bodies, and easy sex." Wade (2017) is convinced that the college hookup culture is deeply intertwined with Greek life, the social fraternities and sororities on college campuses. To understand this relationship between hookups and Greek life, it is important to acknowledge the genesis of these organizations and them becoming an integral part of college life in the United States (Torbenson, 2009).

Fraternities originated in college campuses as early as the 1880s. The purpose of fraternities was to serve as a place for extra-curricular activities where students could unwind after a long day of academic training in classrooms. In those days, fraternities provided a safe space for college men to congregate and debate on Greek texts and other materials that did not find their place in class curricula. It is from these Greek texts that fraternities borrowed the Greek letters, each letter symbolizing intellectual principles. Phi Beta Kappa became the first fraternity to be initiated in 1776 on the campus of William and Mary College. In 1867, the first women's sorority, Pi Beta Phi, was formed at Monmouth College. Over the years, more fraternities and sororities started emerging in college campuses throughout the United States.

Universities eventually granted these Greek organizations the right to own their own houses on college grounds. The fraternity and sorority alumni usually paid for these houses. Besides providing a space for extra-curricular activities, these houses provided an alternate location for students to stay, especially the ones who could not be accommodated in college dorms. For this reason, college administrations became vested in the maintenance of these Greek organizations because these Greek houses saved the college administration money which they would otherwise have to spend to build extra dorms. The generous monetary donation made by the fraternity and sorority alum was another reason why college administrations supported the Greek life growth on campus.

Because of these economic gains, college administrations have consistently been lenient in their monitoring of fraternity and sororities. This has led to Greek organizations being able to arrange parties on school property with near impunity. These parties are usually hosted in fraternity compared to sorority houses, and almost always involve alcohol. This alcohol is usually paid for by the students of the fraternity owing to the significant monetary endowments they receive from their own families and their alumni. Members of other social Greek organizations have access to these parties. However, for non-Greek members, there is a significant amount of gatekeeping that is practiced by these Greek members. As Pham (2017) suggested, access to these parties is limited "to those who possess particular forms of social and gendered capital." Wade (2017) elaborated on this social and gendered capital by suggesting that only physically attractive women (gender capital) and men who could bring more women (social capital) are allowed entry to these fraternity parties.

Through the hosting of such parties with flagrant alcohol consumption, fraternities and sororities have created an atmosphere on campus that is conducive for hookups. Paul and Hayes (2002) found that as many as 44% of college students who had hooked up reported doing so at a Greek party or event. Greek members themselves have a higher rate of hooking up compared to non-Greek members (Owen et al., 2010). This is because every party provides Greek members an opportunity to scout for new hookup partners. Moreover, the alcohol they consume lowers their inhibitions which enable them to make sexual advances with more ease. Greek members are also considered desirable sex partners because of the social status they hold. Thus, non-Greek members may be motivated to hook up with Greek members to enhance their social standing in college. These are the ways in which fraternities and sororities, which started as democratic organizations encouraging intellectual exchange, became breeding grounds of hookups favoring those with social and gender capital.

Athletic Membership

Another group of students who have a higher propensity of hooking up are student athletes, in particular, male student athletes (Allison, 2016). Male student athletes are heralded as "campus elites" who enjoy celebrity-like status especially in college campuses with a strong sports culture. This elevated status increases their sexual desirability which, in turn, increases the odds of them having a greater number of hookup partners. Apart from their social capital, the higher rate of hooking up for male athletes can be attributed to the hypermasculine socialization they experience in their all-male groups. An important part of hypermasculinity is the sexual conquest of women. Therefore, in their attempt to live up to these values and gain a sense of belonging with their teammates, male college athletes may have a strong motivation to engage in short-term sexual relations with multiple women. The picture looks different for female athletes who have been shown to have lower sexual activity than non-athletes. Dodge and Jaccard (2002) analyzed the sexual behaviors of 6,935 female adolescents from middle and high school. They found that the sexual engagement of female athletes was significantly lower compared to non-athletes. Whether this trend exists in college campuses is yet to be examined.

Apart from sociodemographic variables, researchers have also found that students' educational aspirations, their attitude toward sex, and past sexual behaviors also affect their hookup behaviors.

ACADEMIC ACHIEVEMENT
AND CAREER-MINDEDNESS

On average, students need to take 120 credits worth of courses to earn an undergraduate degree. For students who aim to graduate in four years or less, this amounts to 15 credits per semester. For every credit hour, students need to devote at least two to three hours outside of class studying. Such academically oriented students may fear that their grades could be adversely affected if, instead of studying, they spent their time engaging in recreational activities like partying and having casual sex. Therefore, it stands to reason that academically focused students may be more inclined to spend most of their time studying instead of pursuing hookup opportunities. To test this hypothesis, researchers examined the association between GPA (a reliable indicator of academic achievement) and hookup behaviors. Mosley (2009) surveyed 74 college students and found no significant connection between their GPA and their hookup behaviors. This implies that academic achievement may not be related to hooking up; students with high GPAs were just as likely to hook up compared to students with low GPAs.

Apart from academic achievement, researchers have also inquired if academic aspirations or career-mindedness affects students' hookup behaviors. In the Online College Social Life Survey (OCSLS), students were asked about the highest degree they aspired to earn—just a bachelor's degree, a master's degree, or a JD, MD, or PhD. Adkins et al. (2015) analyzed the data from this survey and found that college students' career-mindedness were unrelated to their number of hookup partners.

Stepp (2007) proposed an alternate hypothesis for the effect of career-mindedness on hookup behaviors. She argued that career-minded female college students would avoid relationships that require greater time commitment, and instead engage in short-term sexual relations such as hookups. Fielder and Carey (2010) put this hypothesis to the test by analyzing the hookup behaviors of 140 first-semester college students (109 females, 31 males). They found that career-mindedness did not influence students' sexual behaviors. However, they do caution us about the fact that the first semester of college could be too brief of a time frame to gauge the career-mindedness of students.

SEXUAL PERMISSIVENESS

Sexual permissiveness, people's attitudes associated with sex, has been shown to affect students' hookup intentions and behaviors. Students who are sexually permissive are more likely to hookup, engage in higher-order sexual behaviors like oral and vaginal sex, and have a greater number of sexual partners compared to students who are not permissive (Katz & Schneider, 2013; Olmstead et al., 2013; Townsend & Wasserman, 2011). This association between people's attitudes about sex and their subsequent sexual behaviors can be understood through the lens of Fishben and Ajzen's (1975) Theory of Planned Behavior. According to the theory, if people have favorable attitudes toward a particular behavior, then they are more likely to enact that behavior. Consequently, people who have permissive attitudes toward sex will be more likely to engage in casual sexual encounters, that is, hookups.

The American society has not always been the most sexually permissive. Wells and Twenge (2005) stated that the sexual revolution of the 1960s and the 1970s is when Americans' attitudes toward sex started becoming liberal. Prior to the 1960s, people had restrictive views about sex and considered sex to be appropriate only when it happened between a husband and a wife. Sex outside of marriage was deemed unacceptable, and casual sex was almost heretic. As mentioned earlier, women were judged more harshly than men if they engaged in premarital sex. The introduction of effective contraception and condoms reduced the sexual risks involved for women and men, which helped tilt people's attitudes toward the liberal side. Recently, it was reported that young adults were having less sex than the previous generations (Julian, 2018). This raised concerns about Americans sexual attitudes regressing toward conservatism and the dawn of a sexual counterrevolution. This, however, was debunked by Twenge et al.'s (2015) latest meta-analysis assessing people's change in attitudes between 1972 and 2012. They found that Americans' acceptance of non-marital sex increased between the 2000s and 2010s. Even though the overall sexual activity had dwindled, Americans reported having sex with more partners, and had sex with a casual date or pickup or an acquaintance in the last year.

CURRENT STUDY

Before proceeding with the present study, I examined the extent to which the hookup behaviors of the nationally representative sample of 318 college students aligned with the findings of previous research. In particular, I identified which of the reviewed sociodemographic and psychological variables predicted students' hookup partner count.

To accomplish this task, I provided a definition of the term *hookup* in the survey administered to the participants, vis-à-vis,

A hookup is a sexual encounter, usually lasting only one night, between two people who are strangers or brief acquaintances. Some physical interaction is typical but may or may not include sexual intercourse (vaginal or anal). Examples of physical interaction include kissing or making out, breast stimulation, genital stimulation, and oral sex.

Based on the definition they were asked to indicate the total number of people they had hooked up with in their lifetime. 61.6% of students had 1–5 hookup partners, 18.2% had 6–10 hookup partners, 11.6% had 11–20 hookup partners, 4.4% had 21–30 hookup partners, and 4.1% had 31 or more hookup partners. Subsequently, students answered questions that pertained to their sociodemographic information. These sociodemographic details are provided in table 2.1. In sum, the student sample was predominantly single, White, heterosexual, and Christian. Most students were also not affiliated to Greek organizations or athletics.

Multiple one-way ANOVAs and bivariate correlations were conducted to examine the relationship between the number of hookup partners and the sociodemographic and psychological variables. Results showed significant differences in the number of hookups across only two sociodemographic variables: race and Greek life affiliation. First, Latino students had a significantly higher number of hookup partners compared to Black and Asian students. Asian students had lesser hookups than White students. Second, students who were affiliated with Greek organizations had a higher number of hookup partners compared to students who are non-Greek members. Results also showed that the total number of hookup partners was positively correlated to sexual permissiveness and the total number of sexual partners. This means that students who were more sexually permissive and had a greater number of sexual partners also had a higher number of hookup partners.

I performed a hierarchical regression to examine which of the predictor variables significantly explained the variance in the outcome variable. The outcome variable was total number of hookup partners, and the predictor variables were gender, sexual orientation, race, religion, religious attendance, Greek membership, Varsity membership, GPA, academic aspirations, sexual permissiveness, and the number of sexual partners. According to the results, the number of hookup partners was significantly predicted by Greek membership, race, academic ambition, sexual permissiveness, and the number of sexual partners. Students who belonged to Greek organizations were sexually permissive and who had a greater number of sexual partners were also had a higher number of hookup partners. On the other hand, students who had high aspirations and who are Asian had a lower number of hookup partners compared to White students.

Table 2.1   The Demographic Characteristics of the Nationally Representative College Participant Sample of 318 Students

	Total (N = 318)
Biological Sex	
Male	140
Female	178
Sexual Orientation	
Heterosexual	233
Homosexual	33
Bisexual	52
Race	
Caucasian/White	157
African American/Black	55
Asian	55
Hispanic	40
Other	11
Seniority in School	
Freshmen	62
Sophomore	80
Junior	79
Senior	57
Graduate	40
Religion	
Christian	133
Atheist/Agonistic	102
Religious minorities	82
Religious Attendance	
Never	116
Rarely	114
Regularly	88
Varsity	
Athletes	66
Non-athletes	252
Greek Life	
Greek affiliate	76
Non-Greek affiliate	242
Nationality	
Born in the United States	276
Not born in the United States	42
Relationship Status	
Single	191
Casual Dating	38
In a relationship	89
Academic Ambition	
Bachelors	129
Masters	111
PhD and above	78

IMPLICATIONS OF RESULTS ON
CURRENT HOOKUP CULTURE

The results of the study, by and large, were consistent with previous research in terms of race, Greek membership, sexual permissiveness, and the number of sexual partners. Students who belonged to fraternities and sororities, had liberal attitudes toward sex, and who engaged in sexual behaviors in the past tended to have a higher number of hookup partners. The association between career-mindedness and the number of hookup partners were inconsistent with prior studies that have found no association between these two factors. Findings of this study suggested that students who aspired for advanced academic degrees such as Masters' and PhD had fewer hookup partners compared to students who aspired for just a Bachelors' degree. This lends support to the hypothesis that career-minded students have a lower engagement in the hookup culture, and instead devote time toward their pursuing academic excellence.

In terms of non-significant predictors, some of the results corroborated previous research while others challenged them. First, it was found that female college students had as many hookup partners as male college students. This finding refutes both sexual strategies theory and sexual double standard. This has two implications: (a) college women were just as likely as college men to engage in hookups and (b) college women are not shying away from hooking up out of fear of their reputation being slandered. The fact that women hooking up without the fear of retribution is indicative of the cultural shift that is taking place. This cultural shift, in large part, is fueled by the feminist movement that are empowering women to claim their sexuality without being apologetic for it. Media representations echoing a similar sentiment also play a significant role in changing the cultural narrative. Take, for example, *Slutwalk*, an initiative by Amber Rose to combat slut-shaming and other gender inequality issues. Another example is the massively popular song *Wet Ass Pussy* featuring two female artists Cardi B and Meghan Thee Stallion, who are singing about how much they enjoy sex. Albert Bandura's social learning theory states that we learn our behaviors through observation of others' behaviors and that our behaviors are shaped by powerful external forces like the media. To this end, I argue that the frequent media depictions of sex positivity, and reframing words such as *slut* into an emblem of empowerment, is increasing the likelihood of college women hooking up without worrying about their reputation being stigmatized.

Second, results showed that the number of hookup partners did not vary as a function of sexual orientation, meaning LGB students had just as many hookup partners as heterosexual students. According to a recent Gallup poll, more Americans are identifying as lesbian, gay, bisexual, or transgender

(LGBT) now than ever before. According to the poll, 5.6% of adults identified as LGBT, rising from 4.5% in 2017. Thus, sexual minority students today may have a larger pool of potential partners to choose from which increases their odds of accruing more partners. Second, there may be more avenues available to LGBT students to meet sexually compatible partners. One such avenue is queer-based dating apps such as *Grindr*. In fact, a 2012 study found that 76% of Grindr users used the app to find sexual partners.

Lastly, results showed that neither religious affiliation nor religious attendance affected students' rate of hooking up. One explanation can be that students' need to conform to college hookup culture norms overrides their religiously motivated desire to stay celibate. Alternately, students may no longer view sexual chastity as a parameter of their religious devotion, and thus partake in the hookup culture without any cognitive dissonance.

Overall, the findings suggested that the nationally representative sample of this study, more or less, mirrored the general trends in hookup behaviors within the collegiate context.

MAIN TAKEAWAYS

- The gender difference in the number of hookup partners is progressively becoming obsolete.
- Sexual minority students are getting more opportunities to hook up either because of a larger pool of potential partners or the availability of more venues where they can find potential partners.
- Religiosity does not deter students from hooking up.
- Greek memberships, attitudes toward sex, and past sexual behaviors increase students' likelihood of having more hookup partners.
- Career-minded students are less likely to engage in hookups.

Chapter 3

Meeting Context for Hookups

Parties, School, Dating Apps, and Work

The most stereotypical image that comes to mind when discussing college hookups is that of an alcohol-soaked fraternity party where college students engage in sexually charged dancing followed by making out and moving to a private location to hook up. Although there is much truth to this image— college students do cite parties as a popular venue for hookups—it is not the only place to meet hookup partners. Take the results of the Online College Social Life Survey (OCSLS) that documented the hookup experiences of 12,065 college students. 29% of these students reported meeting their hookup partners at parties. Compared to this, 37% of students reported meeting their hookup partners in school settings (classes, dormitories, or student clubs). School settings and parties have consistently been the two most popular venues of meeting hookup partners for college students. Apart from these two avenues, college students reported meeting hookup partners through high school connections, from their neighborhood and from work. One of the least cited contexts of meeting hookup partners was through online venues—only 2.35% out of 12,065 students reported hooking up with someone they met online or personal ads.

The reason why an extremely small percentage of students reported the Internet as a meeting context for hookup partners can be attributed to the fact that this survey was based on data collected between 2005 and 2011. Significant changes have occurred in the social life of college students since then. Of particular significance is the infiltration of online dating apps such as *Tinder* in college campuses. Since online dating started gaining popularity among the college student population around 2010, the OCSLS survey could not account for the use of *Tinder* or similar apps by college students.

SHIFT FROM OFFLINE TO
ONLINE MEETING CONTEXTS

Entertainer Aziz Ansari and sociologist Eric Klinenberg (2015) in their highly acclaimed book *Modern Romance* argued that online dating is progressively displacing traditional or offline means of meeting partners. They based this observation on the results of Rosenfeld and Thomas's (2012) study titled *How Couples Meet and Stay Together* who surveyed a nationally representative sample of 4,002 Americans. Results showed that, during the 1990s and earlier, none of the heterosexual couples reported meeting their partners online. This scenario changed dramatically between 1995 and 2005 when that number jumped from 0% to 22%. By 2009, the Internet became the third most popular place for couples to meet each other. The shift from offline to online meeting context was even more pronounced for same-sex couples—60% of same-sex couples who had met each other between 2008 and 2009 reported meeting their partners online. Today, the Internet has become the most popular meeting context for both same-sex and opposite-sex couples, officially displacing replacing friends and family as social intermediaries for meeting partners (Rosenfeld, Thomas, & Hausen, 2019).

Online Spaces as Venues for Sex

Research has shown that this trend of meeting people online compared to offline is not only limited to romantic partnerships; people have also used the Internet to find casual sex partners. Peter and Valkenburg (2007) asked 729 adults, "How often do you currently look for sexual contacts on the internet?" Results showed that of 729 adults, only 1% *frequently* sought sex partners online, 5% *sometimes* did, 3% *almost never* did, and 91% *never* looked for sex partners online. This low percentage of people looking for casual sex online could have been because of the lack of centralized and dedicated online spaces where people who were looking to have casual sex with another could congregate solely for that purpose. The physical and health risks associated with having sex with strangers met through the Internet could have also contributed to the low count.

Back in the late 1990s and early 2000s, "on the Internet" meant avenues such as chatrooms, bulletin boards, and first-generation gaming communities MUDs (Multiple User Dimensions) and MOOs (MUD, object oriented). Most of these avenues were not meant to serve as meeting spots to find sex partners. Instead, Internet users adapted these spaces to fit their need to find casual sex partners. The anonymous nature of the Internet made it conducive for people to use it as a space to satisfy their carnal needs. During this time in Internet history, it was near impossible to verify people's online identity and anchor it to their real-life identities. People found a sense of liberation through Internet's anonymity to freely express themselves without any fear of societal retribution. As Turkle (1995), in her book *Life On The Screen: Identity in the Age of the Internet*, explained,

> You can be whoever you want to be. You can completely redefine yourself if you want. You don't have to worry about the slots other people put you in as much. They don't look at your body and make assumptions. They don't hear your accent and make assumptions. All they see are your words. (p. 184)

The freedom warranted by Internet's anonymity turned into a double-edged sword as users started engaging in a myriad of maladaptive behaviors. One of these behaviors was *catfishing*, creating fake online personalities or falsely assuming other's identities (Waring, 2018). In the same book, Turkle (1995) reported one such instance where an individual named Gordon created not one but multiple online characters. While Gordon was a reclusive male college student, his characters were older, self-confident, and extravagant; one of his characters was even a flirtatious female. Gordon is one of the many examples of Internet users deceiving others using the cloak of Internet's anonymity (Caspi & Gorsky, 2006).

Apart from being deceived, pursuing sexual relations with people met on the Internet also came with significant health risks. Bull and McFarlane (2000) observed conversations in 175 online chatrooms, most of which were hosted on the then-popular Internet service provider America Online (AOL). Findings showed that people in these chatrooms frequently made references to risky sexual behaviors such as anal sex, oral sex, and sex with multiple partners and rarely discussed topics of STI prevention.

The online space has transformed significantly since the early 2000s. First, the anonymity of the Internet has substantially reduced with the rise of social networking sites like *Myspace* (now defunct) and *Facebook*. These websites allowed Internet users to transition their offline social networks (people who know them in real life) into the online space while retaining the original essence of the Internet as being a space for forming new relationships with strangers. Since users now had their offline networks present on these websites, they could not fabricate their entire personalities. Instead, users started engaging in what Walther (1996) describes as *selective self-presentation*, that is, strategically portraying themselves in the most positive light possible. Some of the ways in which users practiced selective self-presentation were using airbrushed photographs of themselves, highlighting their personal and professional achievements, and broadcasting their tastes, interests, and memberships in prestigious groups (Fox & Vendemia, 2016; Johnson & Ranzini, 2018; Lee-Won et al., 2014).

Online Dating Transforming the Online Space for Sex

Another turning point in Internet history, along with social networking sites, has been the emergence of online dating platforms (websites and mobile applications or apps) such as *PlentyofFish* and *Tinder*. Similar to social networking sites, users of online dating platforms create their dating profiles where they often engage in positive self-presentation to attract desirable dating partners (Ellison, Heino, & Gibbs, 2008). These platforms allow users to articulate their partner preferences based on which either users can select dating partners on their own or the dating platforms curate a list of compatible partners for the users (Tong, Hancock, & Slatcher, 2016).

Although these online dating platforms are meant to facilitate the process of courtship and dating, people have used them for other reasons. These include using these platforms for fun and entertainment, for forming friendships, and even for seeking out partners for casual sex (Sumter, Vandenbosch, & Ligtenberg, 2017). Online dating platforms as a venue for casual sex is different from previous anonymous online spaces in two ways. First, some online dating platforms come with a clear expectation that they are popular spaces for seeking out casual sex partners. Second, the chances of catfishing others are lower in online dating platforms compared to previous anonymous online spaces. This is because, in most cases, online dating platforms verify users' identities using their existing social networking profiles.

Despite these fundamental differences, the apprehension of engaging in sexual liaisons with complete strangers met online persists in online dating spaces. This is evidenced by the low percentage of people using *Tinder* for casual sex even though the app has earned a reputation of being a *hook up app*. Sumter and Vandenbosch (2019) surveyed 541 Dutch adults to inquire about their dating app use. Results showed that 88% of the Dutch adults reported using *Tinder*. The most popular reason for using *Tinder* was for fun and to find romantic partners. Similar trends in Tinder use have been found in the United States. Griffin et al. (2018) surveyed 409 American heterosexual college students and found that only 4% used *Tinder* for casual sex, and most students used the app for fun and to meet people.

WHO HOOKS UP ONLINE?

Even though college students may not frequently use *Tinder* for hookups, there is no denying that these dating apps have added a new venue where students can look for hookup partners. This raises the question: Are some college students more predisposed to look for sex partners in certain venues compared to others?

To my knowledge, the only study that has come close to answering this question is *Dating and Hooking Up in College: Meeting Contexts, Sex, and Variation by Gender, Partner's Gender, and Class Standing* by Arielle Kuperberg and Joseph Padgett (2015). The researchers analyzed the data from OCSLS and found significant differences between students who hooked up with partners met through school settings, parties, and through the Internet. Some of their findings were: male and female college students who engaged in same-sex hookups or dates tended to meet their partners through Internet connections, and students who met their partners through the Internet were more likely to turn their encounters to dates compared to students who met their partners through institutional settings. Kuperberg and Padgett (2015) used Mahay and Lauman's (2004) theory of network embeddedness to explain these behavioral tendencies of college students. According to this theory, students who meet their partners through face-to-face settings (such as parties) or through institutional connections (such as school and work) share a higher level of trust and familiarity compared to students who meet their partners through Internet connections. These higher levels of trust and familiarity increase students' likelihood of engaging in riskier sexual behaviors. For this reason, students are more likely to hook up with partners met at parties, bars, and dormitories compared to partners met online.

Kuperberg and Padgett's (2015) study demonstrated the importance of recognizing different meeting contexts to gain a more nuanced understanding of college hookups. However, their study did not address two important issues. First, the researchers did not include the psychological factors that have been shown to distinguish individuals who look for casual sex partners online from individuals who look for casual sex partners through traditional offline means. Second, the researchers treated the online meeting context as a monolith without acknowledging the unique nature of online dating platforms. In the following section, I address both these issues.

Compensation, Recreation, and Rich-Get-Richer Hypotheses

Peter and Valkenburg (2007) in their study *Who looks for casual dates on the Internet? A test of the compensation and the recreation hypotheses* proposed two hypotheses to identify the psychological antecedents of seeking casual sex partners met through the Internet.

The first hypothesis, known as the *compensation hypothesis*, states that individuals who have high dating anxiety will use the Internet to compensate for their lack of face-to-face interactional competence, and thus be more likely to meet their hookup partners online. Dating anxiety is defined as the distress one feels in novel dating situations (Glickman & La Greca, 2010). This distress manifests in physical mannerisms as highly anxious people are unable to maintain appropriate eye contact, unable to hold conversations, and overall fail in making a positive impression on their potential dating partners. These individuals, therefore, have a higher motivation of leveraging the gating features of the Internet to compensate for their deficits in face-to-face interactions. Peter and Valkenburg specify three online features that high dating anxious people use to their advantage: (a) limited cues, (b) relative anonymity, and (c) strategic self-presentation.

Face-to-face interactions permit the exchange of more verbal and nonverbal cues compared to online interactions. To put it another way, in face-to-face interactions, one can use all five senses (touch, sight, hearing, smell, and taste), and one is expected to provide immediate verbal or nonverbal feedback. Online communication platforms are bereft of olfactory and haptic cues, and the permissibility of visual and auditory cues varies depends on the modality of the online platforms. For instance, texting has limited auditory and visual cues and may be asynchronous; video calls using Facetime or other similar services allow auditory and visual cues and are synchronous in nature. Apps such as *Tinder* give its users both options—video calling their potential partners or just texting their potential dating partners. Depending on the extent of dating anxiety, app users can choose the communication option that best suits their comfort level.

Online communication also permits a greater degree of anonymity compared to face-to-face interactions. Similar to visual and auditory cues, the degree of anonymity also depends on the modality of the online communication platform being used. People can remain relatively more anonymous on chat forums such as *Omegle* and *Reddit* compared to dating platforms such as *Tinder* and *Hinge*. Even though these platforms do not provide a high level of anonymity, communicating with potential partners through the shield of virtual dating profiles may provide psychological distance to people with high dating anxiety. This, in turn, can increase their confidence in discussing sensitive and socially tabooed topics and can help them make sexual advancements, something they may not have been able to do comfortably in face-to-face interactions.

Finally, online communication gives people with high dating anxiety a chance to engage in strategic self-presentation to create a positive impression on their dating partners. They can do so by selecting photos and highlighting information that presents them in a desirable fashion. The asynchronous nature of online chats permitted by these apps also provide people with high dating anxiety the time needed to edit their responses during conversations. This time lag is not available during synchronous face-to-face interactions.

The second hypothesis, known as the *recreation hypothesis*, states that people who use online means to meet partners are more sexually permissive and have a higher need for sensation seeking compared to people who meet their partners offline. As discussed in chapter 2, people who have permissive attitudes toward sex are more open to unconventional sexual experiences and accepting of nonmarital sex compared to people who have restrictive attitudes toward sex. Since using the Internet to find sex partners is a departure from the norm, it is contended that sexually permissive people will be more likely to meet partners online compared to offline. High sensation seekers are also more accepting of casual sex, have more casual sexual partners, and consume more sexually explicit materials online. Consequently, they are also more willing to go on dates with someone they have met online and engage in sexual relations with them.

Valkenburg and Peter (2007) found support for the recreation hypothesis but not the compensation hypothesis. In other words, people who are sexually permissive and are high sensation seekers were likely to look for casual sexual relations online *and* offline. The support for the recreation hypothesis showed that the same characteristics that predict offline behavior also predict online behaviors. This finding shows that the Internet does not change people's predilections, but it just amplifies them. The lack of support for the compensation hypothesis demonstrated that people with dating anxiety did not use the Internet to compensate for their social ineptitude.

Subsequent scholars have tested these two hypotheses within the context of online dating. Sumter and Vandenbosch's (2019) analysis of 541 Dutch dating app users garnered partial support for the recreation hypothesis as sexual permissiveness predicted people's likelihood of using Tinder for casual sex, but sensation seeking did not. They did not find support for the compensation hypothesis because dating anxiety did not have any association with the use of apps for casual sex. On the contrary, they found that people with low dating anxiety were more likely to use dating apps compared to people with high dating anxiety. This rendered support for what they called the *rich-get-richer hypothesis* according to which people who are socially competent in the offline world will also be more successful in their interactions in the online world. Only one other study has shown support for this *rich-get-richer hypothesis*: Valkenburg and Peter's (2007) study where they identify antecedents of online dating website use.

Besides sexual permissiveness, sensation seeking, and dating anxiety, another factor that has been associated with seeking casual sex online is sexual disgust. Sexual disgust is disgust that is elicited toward sexual partners and toward certain sexual acts. To measure sexual disgust, researchers ask participants to indicate their disgust toward sexual acts such as having anal sex, performing oral sex, or bringing someone one just met back to their rooms to have sex (Tybur, Lieberman, & Griskevicius, 2009). This physiological reaction is intended to deter individuals from participating in suboptimal sexual behaviors with unfit partners that hamper long-term reproductive success. Short-term mating strategies, such as casual sex and hooking up, involve sexual contact with multiple partners that increase the risk of contracting STIs and unplanned pregnancies. People with high sexual disgust may feel repulsed by the idea of exposing themselves to situations that compromise their health and jeopardize genetic success. Alshawaf, Lewis, and Buff (2015) found that people with high sexual disgust were indeed less likely to engage in short-term mating compared to people with low sexual disgust. In terms of dating app use, Sevi (2019) showed that high levels of sexual disgust suppressed people's likelihood of using apps for finding sexual partners. People with high sexual disgust are also uncomfortable with having sex with others before accruing sufficient information about their health and hygiene status. Since the level of familiarity with partners met through online means is typically less than partners met through offline means, this can further suppress the likelihood of people with high levels of sexual disgust to use dating apps for hookups.

CURRENT STUDY

In this study, I aimed to account for a potential shift in preferences among college students in terms of selecting the venue through which they meet their hookup partners. Specifically, I wanted to find if there has been an increase in the number of students reporting meeting their hookup partners through dating apps such as *Tinder* or *Bumble* since the large-scale nationally representative OCSLS. I also wanted to examine if students who choose to meet their hookup partners through online means like dating apps fundamentally differ from students who meet through other meeting contexts, and if so, what were those distinguishing factors?

To answer these questions, I provided students with the definition of the term *hookup*. If you recall from previous chapters, hookups were defined as sexual encounters, usually lasting only one night, between two people who are strangers or brief acquaintances. Some physical interactions were typical but may or may not include sexual intercourse (vaginal or anal). Examples of physical interaction include kissing or making out, breast stimulation, genital stimulation, and oral sex.

Based on this definition they were asked to indicate the total number of people that had ever hooked up with in their lives. Most students reported hooking up having between 1 and 10 hookup partners. Following this, they responded to the question, "Where did you meet a majority of the people that you have hooked up with?" Out of 318 students, 40% students reported meeting most of their hookup partners in school settings (in class, in dorms, or at student clubs), 25% reported meeting most of their hookup partners through online dating apps, 21% met most of their hookup partners in parties or nightclubs, and 14% met most of their hookup partners at work. These results show that (a) school is still one of the most popular meeting contexts for hookups among students and (b) dating apps are progressively becoming a popular avenue for meeting hookup partners.

To determine the factors that distinguish students who meet their hookup partners through the four meeting contexts—dating apps, parties, school settings, and work—I ran multiple Chi-square and one-way ANOVA statistical tests using several demographic and psychosocial predictors. I selected these predictors based on the review of literature provided earlier in this chapter.

Results of these analyses revealed 10 significant factors: age, sexual orientation, varsity, relationship status, sexual permissiveness, sexual disgust, number of hookup partners, number of sexual partners, porn consumption, and masturbation. Each of these factors and their association with the meeting contexts are discussed below:

1. *Age:* Students who were older tended to meet their hook up partners through work compared to parties, school, and dating apps.
2. *Sexual Orientation*: The most popular meeting context for heterosexual students was school followed by parties—43% of heterosexual students met their partners in school and 23% met their partners at parties. For homosexual students, the most popular meeting context for hookups was dating apps—61% of homosexual students met their hookup partners through dating apps and 21% met their hookup partners from school. Bisexual students were partly similar to homosexual students in that dating apps were a popular meeting context for meeting hookup partners; 27% met their hookup partners through dating apps. However, unlike homosexual students, the most popular meeting context for bisexual students was school with 39% meeting their hookup partners through this meeting context.
3. *Varsity*: Both varsity and non-varsity students were more likely to meet their hookup partners through school and parties. However, 30% of non-varsity students met their partners through dating apps compared to only 6.1% of varsity students. This shows that varsity students rarely hooked up with people they met on dating apps.
4. *Relationship Status:* Single students as well as students in committed relationships reported meeting most of their hookup partners through school followed by dating apps, parties, and other locations. However, most students who were casually dating (42%) met their hookup partners through parties followed by dating apps, school, and other location.
5. *Sexual Permissiveness and Sexual Disgust:* Students who met most of their hookup partners through dating apps had higher sexual permissiveness

and lower sexual disgust compared to students who met most of their hookup partners at parties and school.

6. *Masturbation and Porn Consumption*: Students who met most of their hookup partners through dating apps had the highest frequency of masturbation and porn consumption than students who met most of their hookup partners at parties, in school, and other settings.

7. *Number of Hookups and Number of Sexual Partners*: Students who met most of their hookup partners through school had a significantly lower number of total hookup partners and sexual partners compared to students who met their hookup partners through parties, dating apps, and work.

Based on these findings, I have summarized the distinguishing characteristics of students per meeting context in table 3.1:

PERCEIVED BENEFITS AND RISKS ASSOCIATED WITH MEETING CONTEXTS

Besides identifying the demographic and psychological factors that distinguished students who met their partners online versus through offline means, I also wanted to understand the benefits and risks that college students associate with each meeting context. To accomplish this, I asked them two follow up questions. "What are some benefits/advantages of meeting hookup partners in this way? You can mention up to 5 reasons," and "What are some risks/disadvantages of meeting hookup partners in this way? You can mention up to 5 reasons." A qualitative analysis of their responses revealed the

Table 3.1   Characteristics Distinguishing Students Who Hookup through Dating Apps, School, Parties, and Work

Dating Apps	School	Parties	Work
Same-sex hookups	Opposite-sex hookups	Opposite-sex hookups	Age
Non-Varsity	Low sexual permissiveness	Casually dating	
High sexual permissiveness	Fewer sexual and hookup partners	Low sexual disgust	
Frequent porn consumption			
Frequent masturbation			
Low sexual disgust			
More sexual and hookup partners			

benefits and risks college students commonly associate with each meeting context.

Benefits and Risks of Meeting Hookup Partners at School

The biggest benefit of meeting hookup partners through school settings was the possibility of developing friendship with their hookup partners and continuing that friendship beyond hooking up with them. Sharing the same classes and living spaces allowed students to meet and spend time with their hookup partners on a regular basis. Sharing the same classes and living spaces also meant that students shared a lot of common ground with their hookup partners. Having this common ground took away the awkwardness that is inherent in the acquaintanceship process; it allowed students to have easy-flowing conversations. These conversations coupled with time spent together increased the comfort they felt around each other which subsequently aided the hookup initiation.

Ironically, familiarity and repeated interactions were also cited as the biggest disadvantage of meeting hookup partners through school settings. Multiple students mentioned that if things did not work out with their hookup partners, they would be forced to see them every day that would make things very *awkward*. The other concerns students had about hooking up with someone from school were: (a) they were worried that a fallout with their hookup partners could hamper their academic performance, (b) they were worried about "being caught" (they treated hooking up with someone from school as a clandestine affair, something they did not want to disclose to their friends), and (c) they were concerned about spreading of rumors and gossip mills.

Benefits and Risks of Meeting Hookup Partners at Parties

Parties provided students a fun and relaxed environment to meet hookup partners. Students liked the fact that at parties they can get drunk, dance, and choose from many available partners to hook up with. One student mentioned, "everyone at parties has the same intention," suggesting that students who attend college parties share the belief that everyone present at the parties is willing to hook up. Two-way anonymity, that is, students not knowing their hookup partners and their hookup partners not knowing them, was also a commonly cited benefit of meeting hookup partners at parties. This lack of familiarity meant that students did not have to worry about running into their hookup partners later on, thus avoiding any awkward interactions. Students also enjoyed that hooking up with random strangers at parties provided them with an "exciting backstory"; they liked having an interesting story to tell their friends.

When hooking up with someone at parties and bars, students were most concerned about excessive alcohol consumption and the undesirable consequences of the same. Students feared losing their friends at parties after getting too drunk which meant that their friends could not look out for them. They were also apprehensive of date rape and contracting STIs when hooking up with someone they did not know too much about, that too in an inebriated state. Aside from catching STIs, students also worried about "catching feelings." They feared that if they developed feelings for their hookup partners, because of the inherent fun and casual nature of their encounter, those feelings would not be reciprocated. To sum up, students deemed hooking up with someone they met at parties as unsafe because of the risk of sexual assault, STI contraction, and lack of romantic reciprocity.

Benefits and Risks of Meeting Hookup Partners on Dating Apps

The benefits of meeting hookup partners through dating apps were a combination of the benefits of meeting hookup partners at parties and meeting hookup partners in school settings. Similar to parties, dating apps provided students with multiple partners to choose from while remaining partially anonymous. These apps also provided an easy, convenient, and quick way to find hookup partners. Students assumed that everyone on the app had similar intentions—being on the app meant that people were implicitly indicating their willingness to hook up. Dating apps also provided two advantages that students who hooked up with people they met at school cited: (a) proximity to hookup partners and (b) prior knowledge about hookup partners. Since dating apps filter available partners according to distance, students could find partners to hook up with who are close by to them. The profile information and the availability of the "chat" option gave students an opportunity to get to know their hookup partners and also "vet" them by looking them up online to verify their identity. Apart from these benefits, there were two benefits that were unique to dating apps. They were: (a) the possibility of meeting someone they would not have met otherwise and (b) mutual agreement of hooking up. Dating apps provide students with options of hookup partners beyond school affiliation. This allowed students to hook up with people they would not have met under regular circumstances if not for the app. Additionally, students mentioned figuring out their partners' hookup intentions when they chatted with them. As some students mentioned, hookups through apps were "to the point," one student went so far to say that apps were "the fastest way to hook up."

"Catfish" and "dangerous" were the two words most used by students when asked to comment about the risks of hooking up with someone they met through apps. Students were mostly concerned about the accuracy of the pictures that people used on dating apps. They were also anxious about situations where they may have liked the digital portrayal of their partners more than the partners themselves. Students even worried that some people may use a completely fake identity. Thus, going over to someone's place they barely knew or having them come over to theirs made the hookups seem dangerous to students. By doing so, they mentioned running the risking getting kidnapped, murdered, or opening the possibility of being stalked. Risk of STIs was also a dominant concern among students who hooked up with people they met on dating apps.

Benefits and Risks of Meeting Hookup Partners through Work

There were significantly fewer students who hooked up with someone they met at work. This could be because most of the students did not work and went to school full time. The benefits and risks associated with this meeting context were similar to those of school settings. The benefits were proximity and convenience of location to hookup, prior knowledge about hookup partners, and being more safe than other meeting contexts. The disadvantages were awkward run-ins if things did not work out and also the possibility of rumors and gossip.

IMPLICATIONS OF RESULTS ON CURRENT HOOKUP CULTURE

In this section of the research study, I accounted for the different meeting contexts students meet their hookup partners. In particular, I demonstrated the shift that has occurred in college students' preferences of meeting their hookup partners through certain venues over others. Results of my analysis showed that dating apps such as *Tinder* and *Bumble* are emerging as popular venues for college students to meet their hookup partners—25% of 318 students reported meeting most of their hookup partners through dating apps. This marks a significant increase from the results of previous studies that have shown only a small percentage of students meeting their partners through online venues (Kuperberg & Padgett, 2015). Consistent with previous studies, I found that a sizeable percentage of students were still meeting their partners through school and parties, venues that have traditionally been popular among the college population.

Previous research has repeatedly shown that individuals who prefer meeting partners (romantic, social, or sexual) through online venues are different from individuals who prefer to meet their partners through conventional face-to-face contexts. Based on this, I examined the demographic and psychological factors that distinguish college students who met a majority of their hookup partners through dating apps from those who met their hookup partners through parties, school, or work. The results of this analysis were mostly consistent with previous literature.

Findings suggested that dating apps were popular meeting venues for lesbian, gay, and bisexual (LGB) college students while school and parties were popular meeting venues for heterosexual students. The proclivity of using dating apps to meet hookup partners can be attributed to the popularity of online dating, in general, among the LGB population. A recent Pew Research Study showed that LGB adults were twice as likely to use online dating apps compared to heterosexual adults (55% vs. 28%). The rise of dating apps that cater specifically to this population, such as *Her* and *Grindr*, may have drawn LGB students to use these apps to look for sexual partners. Dating apps like *Tinder* that cater to the general population also allow users to set their partner preferences based on their sexual orientation. Thus, LGB students were also able to use these apps to find hookup partners by utilizing necessary sorting filters. Another factor that may have persuaded LGB students to use dating apps to hook up is the difficulty they face in finding sexually compatible partners through school and parties that tend to be predominantly heterosexual spaces.

Besides sexual orientation, students who met a majority of their hookup partners through dating apps also tended to be more sexually liberal—they held permissive views of sex, were less disgusted by sexually deviant acts, engaged in sexual activities like masturbation and watching porn, and even had a higher number of sexual and hookup partners. Students who met most of their hookup partners through parties were also not easily disgusted by deviant sexual acts. In contrast, students who met a majority of their hookup partners through school tended to be sexually conservative. A potential explanation of these results is that dating apps and parties allow students to enjoy a certain degree of freedom to deviate from social norms, which may not be available to students when they meet their hookup partners through school settings. Dating apps allow students to psychologically and physically detach from their offline personas; on dating apps one might be sexually permissive while being conservative in real lives. Dating apps also allow students to hook up with people who do not belong to their preexisting social networks. Thus, they may be able to indulge in sexually deviant behaviors with these unknown individuals without worrying about any social pushback. In the case of parties, students often report consuming alcohol. Being in an inebriated state may lower their inhibitions which in turn make them more open to sexually deviant behaviors such as having sex with strangers.

The lure of dating apps as a popular hookup venue was also evidenced by students' perceived benefits of meeting hookup partners through these apps. Students liked that dating app–initiated hookups were convenient and unambiguous compared to hookups initiated through other meeting contexts. Meeting hookup partners through school and parties required more effort from students' part as students had to invest more time getting to know their hookup partners and socialize with them. These venues also restricted the number of hookup partners could have at their disposal. Dating apps made this process much easier for students by allowing them access to a seemingly large pool of potential hookup partners, whom students could get to know from their dating profiles. The in-built reputation of some dating apps being hookup apps helped students articulate their hookup intentions with much more clarity and with a lot more ease. They could also be more direct in their solicitations of sex over text-based chats than what they could have done face to face.

Students were also apprehensive of using these apps to hook up because they worried about being deceived or physically harmed by their hookup partners. Even though dating apps take several measures to verify the identity of their users, students were still concerned about being catfished. This concern is not completely unfounded—online daters have been shown to routinely exaggerate their physical and social attractiveness to increase their chances of finding desirable partners and sometimes even completely fabricate their identities (Guadagno et al., 2012). Reports of first date rapes and sexual assaults have also been linked to online dating (bbc.com, 2016). Most of the concerns that students had for using dating apps to hook up indicate an overall lack of trust for their hookup partners.

This lack of trust toward hookup partner and concern for one's own physical safety was also shared by students who met a majority of their hookup partners through parties. Students enjoyed that they could drink alcohol, dance, and hook up with random strangers at parties. They were also worried that drinking too much alcohol and having sex with unknown others would make them vulnerable to sexual assault and even STI contraction. These results show that while students do engage get into sexual encounters with strangers, they are well aware of the negative repercussions this may have on their physical and even mental health.

It is probably this lack of trust and comfort with hookup partners met through dating apps and parties that students still prefer meeting their hookup partners through school settings. Students like knowing their hookup partners in person and spending time with them. This familiarity with their partners not only helps them ease into hookups but also keeps the doors open for future companionship. This finding lends support to a potential transformation of college students' expectations from hookups—college students may no longer be looking at hookups at one-off sexual encounters with strangers. Rather, hookups are becoming repeated sexual encounters with known others with an ambiguous expectation of relational commitment.

MAIN TAKEAWAYS

- Online dating apps such as Tinder are increasingly becoming popular venues for meeting hookup partners; schools and parties remain popular places for meeting hookup partners.
- Same-sex hookups are more popular in dating apps; opposite-sex hookups are more popular in schools and parties.
- Students hooking up with people using dating apps are more sexually liberal compared to students hooking up with people met through school.
- Students' preference of meeting hookup partners at parties, school, work, or through online dating apps is affected by their perceived benefits and risks of each meeting context.

Chapter 4

What Happens during a Hookup?

Analysis of College Students' Hookup Scripts

Coauthored with Lucy Dolcich

Scholars have used Simon and Gagnon's (2003) sexual script theory to discern what happens during a hookup and what distinguishes it from other coupling strategies. To understand sexual script theory, we need to first understand Tomkin's (1987) script theory. Tomkin (1987) argued that just as actors use scripts to know which action to perform next in movies and television, social actors (i.e., people) also use scripts to guide their behaviors in day-to-day social situations. Scripts, consisting of a prescribed sequence of actions, help people make meaning of the social situation and predict other people's behaviors present in that situation. Scripts then become these mutually shared conventions that people use as mental shortcuts to navigate different social situations.

Simon and Gagnon (2003) proposed sexual script theory by applying the tenets of script theory in the context of sexual behaviors. According to this theory, sexual scripts outline the typical sequence of actions and events that should occur in sexual encounters. These scripts help people predict and interpret their own behaviors as well as the behaviors of their partners involved in the sexual encounter. When both parties involved in a sexual encounter adhere to the script, it creates a sense of predictability and common ground which, in turn, leads to interpersonal trust. According to Simon and Gagnon (2003), sexual scripts work in three levels: *cultural*, *interpersonal*, and *intrapsychic*, that is, we ascribe meaning to sexual behaviors from a cultural, interpersonal, and intrapsychic perspective.

CULTURAL SEXUAL SCRIPT

Cultural sexual scripts constitute the global perceptions of sexual encounters. These scripts inform us about the socially sanctioned beliefs and norms surrounding different aspects of sexual encounters: whom to have sex with, what type of sexual behaviors to engage in, in what order to engage in these sexual behaviors, and what meaning to ascribe to the sequence and type of sexual behaviors. People learn about these cultural sexual scripts, not from their own behavior, but from socialization agents such as mass media and interactions with friends.

People rely upon these cultural sexual scripts especially in unfamiliar situations. The more well-known and accessible these scripts are to the public, the greater the public's reliance on these scripts to navigate the unknown terrain. However, Simon and Gagnon suggested that people do not always stick to these cultural scripts, and instead create their own unique sexual scripts through negotiations with their sexual partners.

INTERPERSONAL SEXUAL SCRIPT

Wiederman (2015) stated that cultural sexual scripts offer "the general cast of characters (roles) and the relationship among them" (p. 7). This means that even though cultural sexual scripts are powerful socialization tools, people do not always follow these scripts with precision. Rather, people modify these cultural scripts in a way that caters to their needs. An important factor that affects people's modification of cultural sexual scripts is their own sexual history. For this reason, Simon and Gagnon (2003) contended that interpersonal scripts allow people to play an active role in writing their own unique scripts by negotiating the cultural tenets of sexual scripts and their own sexual experiences. Interpersonal scripts give more agency to people, but they may have to bear a cost for it. When two people follow the same script, it leads to positive outcomes. However, when individuals do not follow the same script, it leads to violation of expectations, which could result in negative outcomes. It follows then that divergent interpersonal sexual scripts germinate unpredictability which can have undesirable repercussions. For this reason, Simon and Gagnon (2003) caution people to make sure that their sexual scripts align with their partners to avoid such pitfalls.

INTRAPSYCHIC SCRIPT

The final level in which sexual scripts work is the intrapsychic level. While the sexual cultural script focuses on the global conventions associated with sexual encounters and the interpersonal script focuses on the mutual negotiation of sexual behaviors during sexual encounters, the intrapsychic script focuses on the internal state of the individuals participating in these sexual encounters. Intrapsychic scripts include the personal motivations, needs, and desires that people have for participating in particular sexual encounters and engaging in particular sexual behaviors. Since the internal state varies from person to person, intrapsychic scripts are much more idiosyncratic and unique in nature compared to cultural scripts. This is not to say that cultural scripts do not influence intrapsychic scripts—the tenets of cultural scripts do influence the reasons why people engage in or refrain from sexual encounters.

HOOKUP SCRIPTS: AN APPLICATION OF SEXUAL SCRIPT THEORY

Multiple studies have used Simon and Gagnon's (2003) sexual script theory to examine hookups (Eaton & Rose, 2012; Eaton et al., 2016; Timmermans & Van den Bulck, 2018). As we have discussed, hookups are brief casual sexual encounters between two individuals. Because of this specific nature of sexual encounters, the scripts followed during hookups have attributes that distinguish them from general sexual scripts (refer to figure 4.1). In this section, I discuss these unique attributes of hookup scripts, particularly hookup scripts followed by American college students.

Similar to the general sexual script, the hookup script also works in three levels: the cultural hookup script is informed by the socially agreed-upon definition of the term hookups; the interpersonal hookup script is informed by studying the actual behaviors of college students as enacted in hookup

Figure 4.1 The Intersection of Social Scripts, Sexual Scripts, and Hookup Scripts.
Source: Created by Author.

episodes; and the intrapsychic hookup script is informed by the motivations that students have for hooking up.

Cultural Hookup Script

To identify the elements of cultural hookup scripts, Timmermans and Jan Van den Bulck (2018) analyzed how sexual encounters were portrayed in 200 episodes of popular US-based television shows. These television shows included situational comedies such as *Friends,* and *The Big Bang Theory*, dramas such as *Grey's Anatomy* and *Gossip Girl*, and comedy dramas such as *Sex and the City* and *Girls*. Results of their content analysis revealed that one-third of the sexual encounters portrayed on screen were hookups. From most to least frequent, these characters were shown to hook up with strangers, acquaintances, friends, and ex-partners. 77% of these scenes showed the characters engaging in oral, vaginal, and anal intercourse, and only 2% of these scenes included the characters using any protection or contraceptives. In most cases, the characters were shown to be in a sober state, they enjoyed the hookups, and they ended up becoming friends or sharing a friends-with-benefits relationship with their hookup partners. The characters rarely got into a committed relationship. To summarize, the cultural script of hookups, as endorsed and promoted by television shows, involves two strangers engaging in higher-order risky sexual acts performed with romantic detachment toward partners and without any expectation of commitment in the future.

Sex-Comedy Movies as a Source of Cultural Hookup Script for College Hookups

The cultural hookup script within the college context has been heavily influenced by sex-comedy movies such as *Van Wilder, American Pie, Superbad, Neighbors,* and *Animal House*. This genre of movies continues to portray college as a fun place where students frequently attend wild parties, usually hosted in fraternity houses, get heavily drunk, and engage in sexual acts with reckless abandon. Research has shown that these movies influence students' expectations from college; students even orient their own behaviors to fit the cultural script propagated by these movies. For instance, Wasylkiw and Currie (2012) found that watching *Animal House* led students to endorse binge drinking and have unfavorable attitude toward studying compared to students who did not watch *Animal House*. Garcia and his colleagues (2012) remind us that even though there are elements of truth in the way movies and television shows depict college life, these depictions are still "exaggerated examples of behaviors that are taken to an extreme for the purposes of media sensationalism and activation of core guttural interests" (p.167).

Peers as a Source of Cultural Hookup Script for College Hookups

Students' social networks also serve as an influential source of cultural hookup script within the college context. The collective understanding of what hookups are and how they should take place can be understood from how students define hookups. As mentioned in chapter 1, several scholars asked college students to explain what they meant by the term *hookups* (Paul et al., 2000; Olmstead et al., 2018). According to their findings, there are three common themes in these student-led definitions: (a) hookups happen outside the context of relationships, (b) hookups can include a variety of sexual behaviors ranging from kissing to penetrative sex, and (c) hookups have no expectation of turning into committed relationships.

Interpersonal Hookup Script

As emphasized by Simon and Gagnon (2003), even though cultural scripts are highly influential, people often tend to use interpersonal scripts to guide their behaviors and predict others' behaviors in social situations. To understand the interpersonal hookup scripts used by college students, Paul and Hayes (2002) conducted a study investigating hookup practices of 187 US-based college students. These students had to recall the last hookup they or their friends had and answer 15 questions based on that hookup. These questions touched upon different facets of the interpersonal hookup script including the relationship they or their friends shared with their hookup partners, the role each partner played during the hookup, the sequence of events that led to the hookup, the sexual behaviors they engaged in during the hookup, their reactions to the hookup, and the type of communication with their partners after the hookup. The researchers created response categories for each of the 15 questions, and then collapsed these response categories into key themes that captured the typical interpersonal hookup script followed by college students.

Some elements of the interpersonal hookup scripts followed by college students were consistent with the cultural hookup script, while others were inconsistent. Consistent with the cultural hookup script promoted by media (Timmermans & Van den Bulck, 2018) (a) a majority of the students reported hooking up with strangers, (b) students engaged in a variety of sexual behaviors with sexual intercourse being the most commonly cited sexual behavior, and (c) only 2% of students reported suggesting a future meeting or communication with their hookup partners.

The interpersonal hookup script followed by college students also featured elements of the cultural hookup script popularized by sex-comedy movies. Participants in Paul and Hayes' (2002) study reported that their hookups were typically unplanned. The most common venue where hookups happened was parties followed by dorms and fraternity houses. The frequently cited behaviors associated with hookups were flirting, winking, talking, drinking alcohol, and dancing. Most of the hookups ended when one person left after hooking up. Lastly, students reported experiencing both positive and negative feelings post hookup. But these feelings predominantly leaned toward negative, especially regret and disappointment.

Subsequent researchers have corroborated and expanded on Paul and Hayes's (2008) results. For example, Bogle (2008), in her book *Unhooked*, documented the hookup experiences of 76 college students between 2001 and 2006. Consistent with Paul and Hayes (2002) results, participants in Bogle's (2008) study also reported that hookups mostly occurred at college parties where students got routinely drunk and engaged in a variety of sexual behaviors with someone they were sexually attracted to. The hookup experience of Lynn (name changed), one of Bogle's (2008) respondents, sums up a typical college hookup experience. Lynn recollected,

Umm, [pauses], well, I'm just trying to think of my experience. Well, one of the nights we had a toga party, it's like an initiation party and everyone gets really drunk and . . . everyone hooked up with everyone else [laughs] and it was just like all crazy and . . . I don't even remember what happened because I was pretty drunk, but I ended up kissing one of the other swimmer guys, that was all that happened. But, later I was like: "Ewww, why did I do that?" But, I don't really remember exactly how it got to that point.

Wade (2017), in her book *American Hookup: The New Culture of Sex on Campus*, added more nuance to these findings. Based on first-hand reports of 110 college students between 2010 and 2015, Wade (2017) compiled a comprehensive five-step script that students follow while hooking up at parties. These five steps are: (a) pregame, (b) grind, (c) initiate a hookup, (d) do . . . something, and (e) establish meaninglessness.

Pregaming is the act of consuming alcohol before going to a party. Students reported pregaming to increase their tolerance for the "gross stage" of the party, the time during the night when everyone makes out with everyone and the party turns into a "sexual mosh pit." Alcohol also acted as "liquid courage," because it lowered students' inhibitions and made them more open to doing things they would not do if sober. One such activity is *grinding*. Respondents in Wade's (2017) study described grinding as "clothed sex with a strangers" and "dry humping." This form of sexualized dancing is common on the dance floors at parties where heterosexual men grab women and start grinding on them without asking for consent. During this time, women look to their friends to know how attractive the person grinding on them is because they themselves are unable to see the person.

One respondent bluntly claimed, *hotness* was the only qualification a person needed to satisfy to be considered hookup worthy. After women get approval from their friends that the person grinding on them is hot or hot *enough*, they turn around and face the person. This gesture of turning around served as women's way of initiating a hookup. Wade (2017) explained, "Turning around isn't just turning around; it's an advance, an invitation to escalate" (p. 39). Following this, students either hooked up on the dance floor or relocated to a private location, based on the physicality of the sexual behaviors they chose to engage in. These sexual behaviors ranged from open mouth kissing and groping to sexual intercourse. The last step was to assert a sense of meaninglessness to the sexual act. Wade (2017) analysis showed that students established meaningless in three ways: (a) by blaming the hookup on the alcohol (the sex was meaningless because they did it in a drunken haze and if they can't remember it doesn't count), (b) limiting the number of times they hooked up with the same person (capping hookups to one time to avoid emotional attachment, i.e., "catching feelings"), and (c) creating emotional distance (by either cutting or limiting interaction with hookup partners).

Evolving Changes in Interpersonal Hookup Scripts

We find some commonalities in the interpersonal hookup scripts found by Paul and Hayes (2002), Bogle (2008), and Wade (2017). According to their results, college students typically (a) hook up at parties, (b) are under the influence of alcohol when hooking up, (c) hook up with previously unknown others, and (d) prefer not to further a relationship with their hookup partners. However, evidence from subsequent research has shown that some parts of these interpersonal scripts have changed.

Meeting Context. Kuperberg and Padgett's (2015) analysis of 12,068 hookups showed that parties, though popular venues, were not the most popular venue for students to meet their hookup partners. Compared to 29.8% of students met their hookup partners at bars and parties, 48.4% of students met their hookup partners through institutional settings (classes, dorms, student clubs, and work). Irrespective of the context through which students met their hookup partners, there were two elements that were common among all hookups: they involved binge drinking and higher-order sexual activities such as oral and vaginal sex. However, the extent of binge drinking and the physicality of sexual behaviors varied across meeting contexts. Kuperberg and Padgett's (2015) results showed that heterosexual students meeting through parties had double the likelihood of binge drinking and 22% more likely to engage in vaginal and anal intercourse compared to students meeting through institutional settings.

Hookup-Partner Relationship. Aside from demonstrating the importance of acknowledging the different meeting contexts for hookups, Kuperberg and Padgett's (2015) analysis also demonstrated changes in interpersonal scripts in terms of students' familiarity with their hookup partners and the number of times they hooked up with their partners. Results of their analysis showed that 52% of students reported knowing their partners very well to moderately well, and they also reported hooking up with their partners on an average of 3.11 times.

Students' expectations of future interactions with their hookup partners have also changed. When asked, "Were you interested in having a romantic relationship with the person you hooked up with after you hooked up?", 68% of students said that they had moderate to high levels of interest in pursuing a romantic relationship with their hookup partners (Kuperberg & Padgett, 2015). Findings from other studies on college hookups have shown similar trends (Owen et al., 2011). This shows that students do not follow complete emotional detachment toward hookup partner as prescribed by the cultural hookup scripts or evidenced by previous versions of interpersonal hookup scripts.

Hookup Scripts Being Similar to Dating Scripts. Some studies have also shown that interpersonal hookup scripts and conventional dating scripts share several common elements. For example, Eaton and Rose (2012) recruited 242 Hispanic students to understand the three types of interpersonal scripts they use: the date script, the hookup script, and the hangout script. The researchers used the cognitive script methodology whereby they asked students to describe, in detail, what usually happened during a date, a hookup, or a hangout. While the researchers could identify dating and hanging out scripts, they could not identify hookup scripts. This is because they could not perform a cognitive script analysis on hookups because of insufficient data—only 28 out of 242 students mentioned hooking up.

Eaton et al. (2016) replicated this study by comparing the dating, hookup, and hangout scripts followed by 224 Hispanic and 316 Caucasian students. The students were provided with the prompt:

We are interested in all kinds of initial romantic (sexual) relationship encounters (e.g., hookups, dates, hanging out, one-night stands, etc.). More specifically, we are interested in the events which occur when going out with someone for the first time. Please describe the most recent time you went out with someone for the first time, using up to 20 actions or events to explain what occurred, from beginning to end.

First, students had to classify their most recent encounter as a date, a hookup, or a hang out. Following this, they were provided with a checklist of

68 action items, and for each item they could check if they had performed it or not (yes/no/maybe). This list of 68 items was based on the 51-item dating script that was formulated by Rose and Frieze (1989). Eaton and Rose (2012) subsequently expanded this script to include additional elements such as *ask for outing, decide what to do, groom and dress,* and *pick other up.*

For an item to be considered as a script element, at least 50% of students should have selected it. According to the results, more than half of the script elements were common between the dating, hangout, and hookup scripts. Some of these common elements were *getting to know each other, complimenting each other, attending event, engaging in physical contact, feeling aroused,* and *asking for another outing.* Even though a majority of the hookup script elements were in common with dating and hang out scripts, there were three elements that were unique to hookup scripts: *drinking alcohol, initiating sex,* and *accepting/having sex.* Based on these results, Eaton et al. (2016) concluded that (a) dates, hookups, and hangouts have a common core script and (b) that dating scripts provide the basic underlying structure of all other types of encounters.

Dating scripts in heterosexual relationships tend to be heavily gendered; the dominant belief is that men are responsible for planning the date, asking women out, and paying for events. Eaton and Rose's (2011) content analysis of heterosexual dating research from the past 35 years showed a "strong presence of gender stereotypes in dating beliefs, scripts, and behaviors" among both men and women to this day (p. 856). Since hookup scripts share a similar core structure with dating scripts, hookups invariably end up being gendered (Eaton et al., 2016).

In sum, findings of recent research studies indicate that (a) students meet hookup partners through various contexts aside from parties, (b) students often drink alcohol during hookups, (c) students often hook up with the same person multiple times, (d) hookups always involve some degree of sexual interaction, and (e) students harbor some degree of romantic interest toward their hookup partners.

CURRENT STUDY

While the series of studies conducted by Kuperberg and Padgett (2015) and Eaton and Rose (2012; Eaton et al., 2016) provide a more accurate version of contemporary interpersonal hookup scripts followed by college students, they still leave several questions unanswered. As we have seen in chapter 3, dating apps are emerging as one of the popular ways of meeting hookup partners. However, none of the prior studies has accounted for hookups initiated through dating apps such as *Tinder.* It is important to investigate if the scripts followed by college students when hooking up with people they met online through dating apps fundamentally differs from the scripts they use when hooking up with people they met offline at parties, school, or work. Second, beyond the level of intoxication and type of sexual behaviors, how do the hookup script elements differ across meeting contexts? And finally, are hookup scripts related to certain meeting contexts more gendered than others?

I expand on previous research by answering these questions in the current study. To do so, I asked students a battery of questions detailing their most recent hookup. These questions pertained to the demographic details about their partners, relationship they shared with their hookup partners, the type of sexual activity engaged in with their partners, and post-hookup interaction with their partners. Second, I also asked them to describe, in detail, all the events that happened on the day/night that led them to finally hook up with their partners. Similar to Eaton and Rose (2012), I performed a cognitive script analysis to identify the elements of hookup scripts. To understand if hookup scripts vary by meeting context, I identified hookup script elements that occurred in some meeting contexts but not in others. Since previous research has shown that scripts can be highly gendered (Eaton et al., 2015), I also examine if and how these interpersonal scripts vary by gender across the four meeting contexts.

Meeting Context. Results showed that out of 318 students, 14% reported meeting their most recent hookup partners at a party, 41% reported meeting their hookup partners in school settings, 33% reported meeting their partners through a mobile dating app, and 12% reported meeting their most recent hookup partners at work. These results show a marked difference compared to Kuperberg and Padgett's (2015) study where only 2.4% of the 12,068 students reported meeting their hookup partners online. In this study, that number has gone up to 33% indicating the burgeoning popularity of dating apps as meeting contexts for hookup partners among the college student population.

Demographic details of hookup partner. Results showed that most students hooked up with someone from the same race. This finding shows that, like romantic relationships, students also had a proclivity for racial homophily in hookups. Most students reported hooking up with a student at the same college or another college. Students who met their hookup partners through dating apps were the most likely to hook up with someone who is not a student.

Familiarity with hookup partner. To gauge the level of familiarity with hookup partners, I asked students seven questions: (a) if they had mutual friends with their hookup partners, (b) how often they interacted with their hookup partners prior to hooking up with them, (c) if they had looked up their partners on social media, (d) added them as connections on social media, (e) exchanged phone numbers, (f) sexted them, and (g) how frequently they hooked up with their partners.

Results showed that students who met through dating apps were the least likely to have overlapping social connections with their hookup partners—only 28% of students who met their hookup partners through dating apps had mutual friends with their hookup partners. In comparison, 74% of students who met their hookup partners through parties, school, and work had mutual friends with their hookup partners.

Students who met their partners through school communicated more frequently with their partners compared to those who met their partners at parties and dating apps. Students who met their partners through work also communicated more with their partners than students who met their partners at parties. On average, over 70% of students had looked up and added their partners on social media and even exchanged phone numbers. In terms of sexting, students who met their hookup partners through work were the most likely to sext, followed by students who met their hookup partners through school and dating apps. Students who met their hookup partners at parties were the least likely to sext. Irrespective of meeting contexts, students reported hooking up more than once with their partners with an average of four times. Aside from partner familiarity, students were also asked to indicate on a five-point Likert-type scale the extent to which they were physically and sexually attracted toward their partners. Irrespective of meeting contexts, students were highly physically and sexually attracted to their hookup partners.

Hookup Planning and Initiation. To understand the spontaneous nature of hookups, I asked students if they and their hookup partners planned to meet or did the hookup just happen. Out of 318 students, 60% reported planning to meet, while 40% mentioned not making any plans. When asked where students had hooked up, only 11% of students reported hooking up at the social event in plain sight, while 89% reported moving to a private location (their room, their partner's room, or another private room). Last, I asked students, between them and their hookup partners, who initiated sexual activities. Female students more often reported their partners initiating hookups compared to male students across all meeting contexts. On the other hand, male students more often reported their partners initiating hookups when they met their partners through parties, school, or work; over 70% of male students who hooked up with people met through dating apps reported their partners initiating the hookup.

Hookup Script Elements. Similar to Eaton and Rose (2012), I asked students to "think about the day/night the hookup happened. Describe, in detail, the events that happened that day/night which led to you two finally hooking up?" I recruited an undergraduate coder to code students' responses using the cognitive script methodology. First, we unitized the responses with each unit being an action performed during the hook up. Next, we labeled each of these units based on the hookup script elements shortlisted by Eaton et al. (2016).

For example, when asked to describe what happened during their most recent hookup, one participant responded,

> We were chatting in class on that day. Afterwards, we were hanging out after class and got dinner. Then, we went back to his dorm and hung out. Then, it happened.

The resulting unitized and labeled version of this script was:

Out of 318 responses, 62 responses needed to be eliminated because students either did not answer or provided incoherent responses which could not be unitized and labeled. Hence, we coded a total of 256 responses. Following the rule set by Bower, Black, Turner (1979) and seconded by Rose and Frieze (1989), an action was considered as a script element if it was mentioned by 25% or more participants. Bower et al. (1979) contended that if one-fourth of people spontaneously mention an action, it can be inferred that this action is part of a consensual script.

I present the findings from the script in the following way—first, I list the script elements (i.e., actions that appeared in 25% of the overall responses). Second, I identify script elements that are unique to the four meeting contexts. Finally, I examine if the script elements differ by gender across all four meeting contexts.

Script Elements across All Meeting Contexts
(Parties, School, Dating Apps, Work)

1. Engage in physical contact: This was the most frequently cited script element—55% of students mentioned engaging in physical contact with their hookup partners. But there was a significant variation in the way students mentioned physical contact. Students used an assortment of words or phrases when discussing physical contact during hookups. Some described the actions they performed clearly, while others used vague terms. We categorized this element based on levels

Table 4.1   Selection of Unit of Analysis and Labels for Cognitive Script Analysis of Students' Hookup Scripts

Unit/Action	Label
We were chatting in class on that day	Joke/talk/laugh
Afterward, we were hanging out after class	Hang out
and got dinner	Eat
Then, we went back to his dorm	Go over to other/Stay after/sleep over
and hung out	Hang out
Then, it happened	Engage in physical contact

of abstraction. When students used the least amount of abstraction, that is, they explicitly mentioned the sexual behavior they participated in, it was coded as Abstraction Level 1. These included "kissing," "fucked," "giving head," and "had sex." When students used words or phrases that had a sexual connotation but could be interpreted to include and exclude different sexual behaviors based on the subjective understanding of the reader, those terms were coded as Abstraction Level 2. These included expressions such as "hooked up" and "made out." Lastly, when students used words that did not have any sexual meaning per se but hinted at the escalation of sexual behaviors, they were coded as Abstraction Level 3. These included phrases such as "then stuff happened," "one thing led to another," and "pick up where we left off."

2. Talk: This was the second most frequently cited hookup script element—47% reported talking with their hookup partners. Talking indicated mediated and unmediated conversations that happened before the hookup or during the hookup between partners. Examples included chatting at a party, making small awkward conversations, or texting or video-calling. Sample responses include,

> Just texted and asked if I wanted to. It was the weekend so I said yea and we met up. I picked him up from his work and we got dinner. Then we went and smoked. And after that we hooked up and I took him back home afterwards.

> We started by talking in his car. Then He kissed me first. We then got into other things. And we ended up fully hooking up. All this happened at night.

> The way we hooked up was I went to my friend's party and he was there. He was pretty good looking and handsome and very loyal like. I went from talking to him for a little bit when my friend said " y'all would look cute together" but I didn't say anything nor did he. She ended up walking away and we were still talking until he grabbed my hand and we leaned in and started kissing . . . yeah. Anyways he finally led me into a private room and that's where it happened.

3. Attend event: This was the third most frequently cited hookup script element—38% of students reported attending an event on the night or day they hooked up. These events could be social events (such as going to parties or bars and attending study groups) or dyadic events (such as going to the café or the theaters). Sample responses include,

> After meeting in October at a fraternity party, we became friends over the course of a few months. We talked almost every day for a few months and

got to know each other. In March we were going to hang out and watch a movie. We watched the movie. Afterwards we hooked up.

We had been texting and Snapchatting every day. We set up a date a few days later in the week. We ended up meeting up at a bar before the setup date and talked for a while with each other and friends. We decided to go back to my place, where we proceeded in awesome sex.

4. Hang out: This was the fourth most frequently cited script element—33% of students reported hanging out with their partners right before hooking up with them. Hang out was considered as any activity where two people spent time doing something together or in a group setting. Unlike attending events, hanging out tended to be less structured, less intentional, and more spontaneous in nature. In most cases, students would simply say "we hung out," and in some cases they would specify what they were doing. Some of these specific activities include walking on the street, chilling or sitting on a couch, taking a nap, and playing online games or card games. Sample responses include,

> I had just watched a scary movie and was alone. I was kinda scared and my roommate was gone. So I texted my guy friend to hang out. He came to my room and we watched Netflix. I became comforted by him and then one thing led to another.

> I texted my friend and told her that I wanna see the girl. Then she told her and that girl agreed. I was so nervous before I met her. Then I went to her dorm and took her then we went out for a coffee. Then we went over to my room and we chilled till midnight.

5. Evaluate other: This was the fifth most cited hookup script element—26% of students reported evaluating their hookup partners. Students evaluated their partners on their looks, on the type of interaction they had with them, on how their meeting or hookup was going so far. Sample responses include,

> It was summer and I was bored. I thought it was attractive that he was smart and from Berkeley. I felt like I had nothing to lose by hooking up with a stranger. He would have no way of finding me and my friends so that also contributed to my attitude that I had nothing to lose. I had no intention of making him my boyfriend and made that clear to him. I ended up being his first kiss and took his virginity so was not a great experience for me.

> That was after some days of chatting we were just talking and we enjoyed it we felt something good between us I told her that I like her she told me the same thing so we ended up hooking.

Meeting Context-Specific Script Elements

Apart from these five actions that qualified as hookup script elements, there were five actions that appeared in 25% or more scripts in some but not all meeting contexts. I list those script elements below.

1. Get to know one another: Students who met their hookup partners at parties, at school, and at work mentioned getting to know their partners before they hooked up with them. Since people primarily get to know each other through conversations, this script element was often conjoined with the script element "talk." Besides conversations, students also reported getting to know one another through social media interactions. Of particular significance in this regard was the utility of the social media platform Snapchat. Sample responses include:

   > We were watching an outdoor movie together. We were lying in a bed of a truck under blankets and spent a lot of time together. We were talking all night and getting to know each other. He made the first move on me at the end of the night.

   > We had been talking for a while. After we had exchanged Snapchats, we would talk on there, send pictures, and video call on Skype. We both admitted our feelings for each other. Then we decided we wanted to go on a date. We decided upon a location that worked for both of us. Then she picked me up and we drove there and had a date.

2. Ask for hookup: Students who met their hookup partners at parties or at work made an explicit request to their partners if they wanted to hook up. The way these requests were made varied in their degree of directness. Some of the requests were direct and unambiguous while others were indirect and covert. A common strategy that students used when propositioning a hookup in an indirect way is asking their hookup partners to hang out or come over to their place. Sample responses of direct and indirect approach to soliciting hookups include:

   > He was a friend of my former boss who was visiting NYC, where I lived. We went out to all the gay bars together, and I realized that this guy worked at the bar across the street from my apartment. We were dancing on the dance floor and he asked if I'd like to hook up with him and I weighed it over and decided: "Yeah! I would like to hook up with him."

   > We had made plans to meet up at a local bar. We spent the night at the bar, but I suggested we go to my other favorite bar. We sat there and drank for a while and flirted. He kissed me. On the way home he asked me if I wanted to come over and I did.

3. Go over to other: Only those students who met their hookup partners at parties mentioned going over to their partners' place. In some cases, this action sequentially follows the element "ask for hook up" in which a request is made to go over to the hookup partners' place. Students acceded to this request, and this action constituted as "go over to other." Sample responses include,

> We met at a bar/club and he asked me to dance. We made out and fooled around on the dance floor all night. When the club closed at 2:00 am, we took a walk. We fooled around some more on the floor of his dojo. Around 4:00 am he drove me to his house and we had sex. I spent the night and we had sex again the next morning before we exchanged numbers and he drove me back to my apartment.

> We had been spending the night off and on for weeks with no sex. Then his fraternity had a party on a Saturday and I decided to go with him/a group of friends. At the end of the party we kind of mutually agreed we would go back to his place. We were both drunk and then ended up hooking up in his room that night.

4. Drink alcohol: Another action that only those students who met their partners at parties reported doing was drinking alcohol. When discussing hookups, past scholars have taken alcohol as a constant that it is always present in hookups. In most cases, students reported their state of inebriation when reporting their alcohol consumption. In some cases, students mentioned drinking alcohol as being a part of a game. Sample responses include:

> Literally have no clue who this guy is other than he added me on Snap after. We were both drunk and he started dancing with me. And after we started dancing we hooked up.

> We were at a house party that got busted by the police. When we were leaving in a big group a bunch of people suggested we get food. At the place we were eating we talked and he asked for my Snapchat. We were both drunk and wide awake and wanted to talk more. Everyone else wanted to leave so he suggested I come back to his dorm and I said sure.

> I broke up with someone. My buddy took me to a party. We played beer pong, met some girls, then ended up making out with them. Made sure they got in an Uber safe, and walked home.

5. Discuss plans: Only those students who met their hookup partners through dating apps reported discussing what they would do during the night or day they met up with their hookup partners. When making plans,

some students decided to meet up exclusively to hook up while others did not vocalize any such explicit expectation. Sample responses include,

> I had been texting him on Grindr for a couple of hours. We swapped pictures and talked about where and when we could hook up for sex. I then gave him my address. He then said he was on his way over. When he got there we had sex.

> We met on Bumble. We decided to meet in person at a Starbucks. Afterwards we went to a Mexican restaurant and he got us tacos. Afterwards we went for a walk and he kissed me. We then decided to go see a movie. We made out during the movie. When the night was over, he dropped me off home and we kissed goodnight.

Based on these results from the cognitive script analyses, I have summarized the interpersonal hookup scripts for each meeting context.

Gender-Specific Scripts per Meeting Context

To find out if hookup scripts tended to be gendered in some meeting contexts compared to others, I examined the hookup script elements at a more granular level. First, I calculated the frequency with which each of the five core hookup script elements (engage in physical contact, talk, attend event, hang out, and evaluate each other) occurred in male versus female hookup scripts. Next, I identified the hookup script elements that occurred in specific meeting contexts for both male and female hookup scripts. Finally, I compared the frequency of these meeting context-specific hookup script elements across gender to understand if hookup scripts tended to be gendered in certain

Table 4.2 Hookup Script Elements That Occurred More than 25% of the Time in Each Meeting Context

Party	School	Dating App	Work
1. Attend Event	1. Attend Event	1. Attend Event	1. Attend Event
2. Get to know one another	2. Get to know one another	2. Talk	2. Get to know one another
3. Talk	3. Talk	3. Hang out	3. Talk
4. Hang out	4. Hang out	4. Evaluate other	4. Hang out
5. Drink Alcohol	5. Evaluate other	5. Discuss Plans	5. Evaluate other
6. Evaluate other	6. Engage in physical contact	6. Engage in physical contact	6. Ask for hookup
7. Ask for hookup			7. Engage in physical contact
8. Go over to other			
9. Engage in physical contact			

Table 4.3 **Hookup Script Elements of Male and Female Students across Four Meeting Contexts (Parties, School, Dating Apps, Work)**

	Male Students	Female Students
Parties	• *Attend event (69%)* • *Talk (62%)* • **Hang out (38%)** • **Evaluate other (38%)** • *Get to know one another (38%)* • *Drink alcohol (31%)* • *Engage in physical contact (62%)* • **Level 1 (25%)** • Level 2 (31%)	• *Attend event (61%)* • *Talk (48%)* • **Go over to other (39%)** • *Get to know one another (32%)* • **Ask for hookup (29%)** • *Drink alcohol (26%)* • *Engage in physical contact (68%)* • Level 2 (31%)
School	• *Attend event (36%)* • *Talk (43%)* • *Hang out (26%)* • *Evaluate other (31%)* • **Eat (26%)** • *Engage in physical contact (52%)* • *Level 3 (26%)*	• *Attend event (33%)* • *Talk (42%)* • *Hang out (33%)* • *Evaluate other (37%)* • **Get to know one another (31%)** • **Go over to other (27%)** • **Discuss plans (25%)** • *Engage in physical contact (71%)* • *Level 3 (40%)*
Dating Apps	• **Attend event (41%)** • *Talk (51%)* • *Discuss plans (38%)* • **Watch movie (32%)** • *Engage in physical contact (70%)* • **Level 1 (27%)** • **Level 3 (32%)**	• **Hang out (57%)** • *Talk (42%)* • *Discuss plans (28%)* • **Move to private location (28%)** • *Engage in physical contact (70%)* • **Level 2 (36%)**
Work	• *Attend event (45%)* • *Talk (55%)* • *Hang out (27%)* • **Evaluate other (45%)** • **Ask for hookup (36%)** • **Discuss plans (27%)** • **Go over to other (27%)** • **Meet at own home (27%)** • *Engage in physical contact (55%)* • **Level 1 (27%)**	• *Attend event (35%)* • *Talk (59%)* • *Hang out (25%)* • **Get to know one another (35%)** • **Watch movie (25%)** • *Engage in physical contact (76%)* • **Level 2 (41%)**

The percentages included beside each script element indicate the frequency with which college students mentioned those elements in their hookup scripts. Elements italicized indicate the frequency of occurrence of script element varying across genders in that specific meeting context. Elements bolded indicate that they appeared in only one gender's hookup scripts in that specific meeting context.

meeting contexts more than others. I have summarized the results of this analysis in table 4.3.

IMPLICATIONS OF RESULTS ON
CURRENT HOOKUP CULTURE

In this section of the study, I added nuance to the existing literature on hookup scripts followed by college students by examining how these scripts differed across meeting contexts.

In addition to that, I also examined if the hookup scripts in certain meeting contexts tended to be more gendered compared to others. In other words, did students perform actions that align with traditional gender roles when meeting hookup partners through parties, school, dating apps, or work?

To accomplish these goals, I asked students a list of questions pertaining to their most recent hookup partners and also the events that transpired during their most recent hookup. Most students met their most recent hookup partners at school, followed by dating apps, parties, and work. On average, students were sexually and physically attracted toward their hookup partners. Students also reported sharing a fair amount of familiarity with their hookup partners. Even though students who met their hookup partners through dating apps did not communicate as often with their hookup partners, they did report sexting their hookup partners compared to students who met their partners through the other three contexts.

The hookup initiation showed a marked gender-specific trend—a majority of male college students reported initiating the sexual activities during hookups compared to female college students. The only exception to this was male college students who hooked up with partners met through apps; a majority of these students reported that their partners initiated the sexual activities during hookup more often than they initiated. Post hoc analyses showed that this happened specifically in same-sex college men hookups.

Results from the cognitive script analyses revealed five elements that were dominant in all hookup scripts, irrespective of meeting contexts: *engage in physical contact, talk, attend event, evaluate other*, and *hang out*. This was mostly consistent with Eaton et al.'s (2016) results where they found that hookup scripts comprised of six elements: *getting to know each other, complimenting each other, attending event, engaging in physical contact, feeling aroused*, and *asking for another outing*. As is evident, some elements such as engaging in physical contact and attending event were common, while others were not. This can either be interpreted as the changing nature of hookup scripts or that some of these elements are highly interrelated to each other.

For example, getting to know each other and talking are highly interrelated, so are evaluating each other and complimenting each other.

I extended previous research on hookup scripts by examining if and how hookup scripts vary based on the context in which students met their hookup partners. Results showed that hookup scripts did differ across meeting contexts as some elements appeared in some meeting contexts but not in others. For example, *drinking alcohol* is a part of the hookup script only when students met their partners at parties. This finding challenges the common assumption that drinking alcohol is a quintessential part of hookup scripts, irrespective of where you meet your hookup partners. Party hookup scripts also included more script elements compared to hookup scripts related to other meeting contexts. Some of these elements were *asking for hookup* (directly or indirectly propositioning hooking up to partners) and *going over to other* (going over to partners' place).

Another element that occurred in all of the meeting contexts except for dating apps was *getting to know one another*. A possible reason why students who met their hookup partners through dating apps did not explicitly mention this element as a part of their hookup script could be because they already get to know their hookup partners by perusing their dating profiles. One element that was unique to the dating app hookup script was *discuss plans* where students made plans to meet up with a clear or vague expectation of hooking up. This finding is in line with Christensen's (2021) proposition that dating app–initiated hookups follow a *hybrid hookup script*, a "contemporary (hetero) sexual script reintroduces traditional dating practices into the hookup script while maintaining the expectation of casual sex" (p. 445). Elements such as *discussing plans* are inherent to dating scripts. However, unlike dating, the expectation in hookup scripts is that those plans will eventuate in some sort of sexual encounter.

Elements like *asking for hookup* and *discussing plans* also indicate that clear communication is becoming a norm during hookups. Instead of passively following ambiguous cues or acting under assumptions, students are prioritizing transparency and clarity with their sexual expectations from their partners. The notions of "enthusiastic consent" and "an unclear response should be taken as a no" among other viewpoints about definite intentions, may be the case of this element being more common. This clear communication is especially apparent with the reporting of the element *discuss plans*. Regardless of gender, people who used dating apps commonly discussed plans with their hookup partners. Based on gender, though, men who met their partners either through dating apps or work, and women who met their partners through either dating apps or school, were likely to report discussing plans with their partners.

Before discussing the gendered nature of hookup scripts, it should be clarified the type of actions that have been traditionally linked to certain genders. Relational actions such as *talking* and *getting to know one another* are considered as female-oriented. In contrast, actions that indicate taking initiative such as *asking for hookup* and *discussing plans* are considered as male-oriented. Keeping this in mind I found some instances where students performed traditional gender role–oriented actions in certain meeting contexts compared to others. At the same time, there were also instances where they defied these gender norms. Meeting contexts where college men performed gender-specific actions were dating apps (discussing plans) and work (asking for hookup). College women performed the gender-specific action of talking and getting to know one another in all meeting contexts (except for dating apps where they did not mention getting to know their partners). College men defied gender norms by engaging in the following actions per meeting context: talk (in all meeting contexts) and getting to know one another (parties). On the other hand, college women defied gender norms by engaging in the following actions per meeting context: discussing plans (dating apps and school) and asking for hookups (parties).

One instance where college men and women adhered to traditional gender role–oriented behavior across meeting contexts was the way in which they discussed physical contact. Overall, college women tended to speak about their physical contact in more abstract terms compared to college men. This tendency of women to avoid discussing physical contact in explicit terms is in line with previous research that claims that women often use the ambiguous nature of the term "hook up" to save their reputation owing to the sexual double standard.

The results of this study show that hookup scripts may not be completely gender egalitarian, but they do tend to be less gendered than dating scripts. The defiance of gender norms by both male and female college students also forces us to reevaluate our long-held beliefs about gender-specific expectations from hooking up. The cultural expectation is that men have a low-investment mentality in hookups. This means that men only care about the end goal of being able to make out or have sex. For this reason, they may not be motivated to talk and spend time with their hookup partners. Gauging compatibility with their partners or assessing the quality of interaction with their partners may also not be a priority for them. But as is evidenced by the results, it has become normative for male college students to perform these actions in hookups. On the flip side, female college students defied traditional gender norms of passively receiving men's actions as they proactively discussed and planned the day or night of the hookup with their hookup partners.

MAIN TAKEAWAYS

- Hookup scripts share common characteristics with dating scripts. They include *engaging in physical contact, talking, attending event, evaluating hookup partners, and hanging out.*
- Hookup scripts are not uniform—they vary based on the context in which college students meet their hookup partners.
- Alcohol is central to hookup scripts only when students meet their hookup partners at parties.
- Dating app–initiated hookups follow a hybrid hookup script.
- Students both conform and defy traditional gender roles in hookup scripts across meeting contexts.

Chapter 5

The Positive and Negative Outcomes of Hooking Up

Researchers who have studied hookups have often led with the assumption that hookups are essentially bad for college students (Fielder & Carey, 2010; Mellins et al., 2017; Owen & Fincham, 2011). The negative bias toward hookups is grounded in the moral panic surrounding hookups, which is that these short-term sexual encounters lead to commitment phobia among young people. Students are less willing to date and more willing to engage in sexual behaviors with others without any promise of exclusivity. Researchers also argued that hookups are physically harmful to students. Since hookups entail students spontaneously engaging in sexual behaviors often under the influence of alcohol, this exacerbates the chance of unprotected sex, unsolicited sexual contact, and worse, sexual assault (Lambert, Kahn, & Apple, 2003).

The alarm bells rung by researchers are not completely unfounded. Multiple studies have shown that hookups are related to negative physical and emotional health outcomes such as STI contraction, unplanned pregnancies, shame, depression, and guilt (Downing-Matibag & Geisinger, 2009; Owen, Fincham, & Moore, 2011). Furthermore, these negative effects have been found to be more acute for college women than men (Paul et al., 2000). However, subsequent research showed that hookups also led to favorable outcomes such as feelings of arousal, sexual satisfaction, and experience of positive emotions such as happiness and excitement (Snapp, Ryu, & Kerr, 2015). In the next section, I review both the negative and the positive physical and emotional consequences of hookups, and how they differ for college men and women. Next, I examine the sexual outcomes reported by students in the present study and identify factors that predict these outcomes. In the end I discuss the extent to which the results of this study are consistent with previous literature, and what implications they hold for the physical and mental well-being of college students.

NEGATIVE OUTCOMES OF HOOKUPS

Health Risks

Hooking up has been associated with risky sexual behaviors, in particular, sexual intercourse without the use of condoms or any other preventative measures. Lewis et al. (2012) found that out of 824 students, 429 had penetrative intercourse (oral, vaginal, or anal) during their most recent hookup. 53.4% of these 429 students reported not using a condom. Despite engaging in risky sex, an overwhelming percentage of young adults believe that they are not at a risk of contracting sexually transmitted diseases (STIs) (Adefuye et al., 2009). Unfortunately, the reality is different and grim. According to a 2018 CDC report, almost half of the 26 million new cases of STI consisted of individuals between the ages of 15 and 24. This collective ignorance creates a false sense of security for college students that makes them more likely to violate safe sex practices.

The lack of using condoms during hookups has been attributed to (a) students' intoxicated state owing to alcohol consumption and substance use, (b) familiarity with hookup partners, and (c) feelings toward partners (Hall et al., 2018; Lambert et al., 2003).

Intoxication

Alcohol. The initial conceptualization of hookups was that these short-term sex acts usually happened at parties between two strangers. Since alcohol and parties go hand in hand, students who attend parties invariably find themselves in a heavily inebriated state resulting from unregulated alcohol consumption. With their inhibitions reduced, students become more open to making sexual advances and engaging in hookup behaviors, which they would have refrained from if sober.

Empirical evidence has supported the hypothesis that alcohol consumption increases students' likelihood of hooking up, and it also affects the level of physicality involved during hookups. For instance, 64% of college students in Fielder and Carey's (2010) study reported consuming an average of three drinks during their hookups. Ross and associates (2015) found that White male college students who reported consuming more alcohol had "more intense hookup experiences" that included touching, oral sex, and vaginal sex compared to participants who did not consume alcohol.

The higher physicality during hookups aided by alcohol consumption, consequently, increases the chances of students having unprotected sex. This causal effect of alcohol on risky sexual behaviors can be explained using Steele and Joseph's (1990) alcohol myopia theory. According to this theory, alcohol increases people's sensitivity to arousal cues while reducing their sensitivity to inhibition cues. In other words, alcohol consumption during hookups enhances students' sexual arousal and impairs their ability to process safety cues such as contraction of STIs and unplanned pregnancies that would ordinarily keep them from engaging in risky sexual behaviors. Alcohol myopia theory (Steele & Joseph, 1990) has been supported by multiple research studies. Downing-Matibag and Geisinger (2009) interviewed 71 college students to gauge the type of risk-taking they practiced during hookups. They found that 81% of students who reported drinking alcohol before or during the hookup confessed that they would not have done what they did, sexually, during their most recent hookup had they been in a sober state. Sheena, one of the participants, reflected, "In my sober mind I would never, ever, have sex without a condom. So, yeah, I think alcohol definitely had a role in that" (p. 1203).

Drug Use. Compared to alcohol consumption, the research on substance use and risky hookup behaviors is sparse. The few studies have examined this issue have garnered mixed results. Studies that have garnered support for the claim that substance use during hookups increases the odds of unprotected sex have mostly been based on high-risk populations. For example, adolescents in detained facilities were more likely to have unprotected sex if they used marijuana during the sexual episodes or used marijuana in general (Kingree, Braithwaite, & Woodring, 2000). Research has also shown that individuals' gender moderates the association between marijuana use and unprotected sex. Adedeji et al. (2009) examined college students' overall marijuana use in the past 30 days and its association with risky sexual behaviors. Results showed that marijuana use increased the chances of inconsistent condom use during sex by five times, but only among female college students. Walsh et al. (2014) conducted a similar study, but instead of accounting for participants' general marijuana use, they checked for the effect of marijuana use during hookups on a sample of 297 college women. In this scenario, no association was found between marijuana use and condom use during their last hookup.

Familiarity with Hookup Partners

Besides alcohol and substance use, another factor that has been associated with risky sexual behaviors during hookups is the level of familiarity between college students and their hookup partners. The underlying assumption in the earliest definitions of hookups was that they were one-off sexual encounters that happened between two people who barely knew each other (Paul et al., 2000). Subsequent research has shown that college students not only hook up with people they know, but they also hookup with the same partner more than once (Fielder & Carey, 2010). This familiarity that students develop with their hookup partners, through repeated interactions and hookups, engenders a level of trust that affects their decision to use condoms during sexual encounters. There are two schools of thought on this matter. Some researchers believe that the interpersonal trust between students and their hookup partners help students negotiate condom use with greater ease. Consistent with this expectation, Lewis et al. (2012) found that college students were more likely to use a condom when hooking up with an ex-partner and casual acquaintance compared to hooking up with a stranger. On the other hand, other scholars insist that the interpersonal trust make students more likely to have condomless sex because they do not view their hookup partners as threats to their physical health. Kuperberg and Padgett (2015) found partial support for their claim—female college students had a greater likelihood of engaging in unprotected sex during their last hookup when they knew their partners really well. However, this association between partner familiarity and unprotected sex was not found among male college students.

Besides partner familiarity, college students' feelings toward hookup partners also interfere with their decision of escalating the degree of physicality and engage in unprotected sex. College students who are sexually attracted toward their hookup partners are more likely to engage in higher-order sexual behaviors such as oral, vaginal, and even anal sex. An 18-year-old male college student in Spencer Olmstead and associates' study (2013) stated, "To me, sex happens when two people are extremely sexually attracted to each other and there is no other way to express this attraction than to have sex."

Feelings toward Hookup Partner

College students' sexual attraction and romantic feelings toward hookup partners have also been shown to affect their likelihood of engaging in risky sexual behaviors during hookups. Even though hookups are supposed to be casual sexual encounters with no expectations of exclusivity or relational commitment, students have often reported romantically desiring their partners. Garcia and Reiber's (2012) study on college students' expectations from hookups showed that 37% of 507 students believed the ideal outcome of a hookup is for it to culminate in a romantic relationship. Since condom use is often seen as an indicator of lack of trust, students who want their hookup partners to turn into their romantic partners may avoid demanding the use of condoms to signal trust in their hookup partners. Hall et al. (2019) analyzed the data from Online College Social Life Survey and found that students who were romantically interested in their hookup partners were more likely to report unprotected penetrative sex than those who did not have any romantic interests in their hookup partners. Jenkins' reports also showed that college women were less likely to use condoms during their last hookup compared to college men. This finding makes sense considering that college women are also more likely to desire romantic relationships with their hookup partners, as reported by Garcia and Reiber (2012).

Sexual Assault

Hookups have also earned a negative reputation for contributing to the occurrence of sexual assault on college campuses. Research on sexual assault, nonconsensual sexual interaction involving force or incapacitation, has mostly focused on female sexual victimization (Berkowitz, 1992). Rightfully so, because the rate of sexual assault on women is much higher than that of men. According to the National Intimate Partner and Sexual Violence Survey conducted by CDC, 1 in 5 women compared to 1 in 71 men in the United States have been raped at some time in their lives.

Female Sexual Victimization

Women attending college have also been shown to face increased vulnerability to sexual assault. Fisher et al. (2010) estimated that around 1 in 5 women (20%) are sexually assaulted during their four years in college. The prevalence of sexual assault toward college women has led researchers to conclude that sexual victimization is a "widely recognized grim reality for a substantial proportion of women during their college tenure" (p. 103). It is alarming that things seem to be getting worse in terms of college female safety since Fisher's 2010 study. A number of recent studies have corroborated the statistic that today, not 1 in 5 but 1 in 4 college women (25%) report being assaulted in college.

Intoxication and Sexual Assault. Flack et al. (2016) recruited 373 undergraduate female students to test the association between hookups and occurrences of sexual assault. According to their results, the most common type of sexual assault during hookups was non-invasive sexual touching, followed by attempt rape and complete rape (oral, vaginal, or anal). Flack and colleagues, along with other researchers, have argued that alcohol consumption, one of the key features of hookups, significantly contributes to sexual assault. In Flack's study (2013), 30% of women mentioned being sexually assaulted while being incapacitated by alcohol.

Along with alcohol, substance use has also been related to sexual assault. The Campus Sexual Assault Study (Krebs et al., 2009) showed that marijuana use increased the odds of college women being victims of incapacitated sexual assault. This tendency of assaulting incapacitated women is related to rape-supportive beliefs that male college students reportedly endorse. Burgess's (2007) study on 368 college men found that college men who accepted rape myths were also more likely to report sexual aggression. Some of the alcohol-related rape myths include:

Women who drink at parties are giving off signal that they are more sexually available than women who do not drink at parties.

If a woman willingly gets drunk, then she is raped—she is more responsible for what happened to her than if she had decided not to drink.

If a man wants to increase his chances of having sex with a woman, he should get her drunk.

It is okay for a man to have sex with a female acquaintance who is drunk.

Heavy drinking and substance use are a common occurrence at college parties. As a result, hookups initiated at parties, particularly parties hosted by fraternities and sororities, have been associated with a greater risk of sexual assault compared to hookups initiated in other meeting contexts (Hines et al., 2012). Krebs et al.'s (2019) results from the Campus Sexual Assault Study showed that college women who attended fraternity parties were more frequently and also more likely to be victims of incapacitated sexual assault.

Male Sexual Victimization

Over the past four decades, scholars have consistently called attention to the sexual assault crisis that plagues American college campuses. Because of the consistent high rates of sexual assault against college women, most of the research studies on campus sexual assault have examined the issue from the standpoint of women being the victims and men being the perpetrators of sexual assault. However, an emerging body of research has shown that college men also experiencing sexual assault, albeit at a lesser rate than college women.

Claude Mellins along with a team of 14 researchers from Columbia University launched the Sexual Health Initiative to Foster Transformation (SHIFT) program to investigate sexual assault incidences among college students. As a part of this program, the researchers recruited 1,671 students from two large universities in New York City: Columbia University and Barnard College. Consistent with extant research, SHIFT reports showed that 28% of college women reported experiencing at least one incident of sexual assault. However, the study also found that 12.5% of college men also reported experiencing sexual assault. Mellins et al.'s (2018) results are not unique to a city-based college population. Forsman (2017) conducted a review of five studies examining sexual assault among college men from both urban and suburban universities. Based on these studies, Forsman concluded that the rate of sexual victimization among college men ranged from 3% to 28%.

At first glance, one may be tempted to believe that college men reporting sexual assault may have experienced the assault in the context of same-sex partnering where the assault perpetrators are still men. It is true that homosexual and bisexual men report a higher rate of sexual assault than heterosexual men (Friedman et al., 2011). At the same time, there is empirical evidence of college men experiencing sexual assault in opposite-sex partnering as well. Findings from Online College Social Life Survey showed that 24.3% and 17.7% of gay and bisexual men experienced sexual assault (Ford & Soto-Marquez, 2016). Results also showed that 12.7% of heterosexual male college students reported being victims of sexual assault. Other researchers have also found similar trends in their data. Hines et al. (2012) found that 3.2% of 535 college men reported experiencing sexual assault, and 73.3% of these college men reported their perpetrators being female.

Intoxication and Sexual Assault. Similar to college women, college men's sexual assaults have also been associated with alcohol consumption. Turchik's (2012) analysis of 302 male college students' sexual assault experiences showed that almost half of the population reported experiencing at least one instance of sexual assault. Results also showed that college men's weekly drinking habits and problematic drinking behaviors (getting sick after drinking, getting DUIs) were positively related to the severity of sexual assault they experienced. The lowest level of severity was unwanted sexual contact, and the highest level of sexual severity was rape. The risk of sexual assault among college men is also exacerbated by their high alcohol consumption. On average, college men consume more alcohol compared to college women— according to a 2014 study, college men consumed an average of seven drinks prior to hooking up compared to college women's average of five drinks (Labrie et al., 2014). This higher level of intoxication invariably puts them at a higher risk of sexual assault compared to their female counterparts.

Attending parties have also been associated with greater risks of sexual assault among college men. Littleton and her colleagues (2020) analyzed the sexual victimization of 58 college men and found that most of men's assaults happened at parties. Furthermore, the most common type of sexual assault to happen to men at college parties was unwanted sexual contact. One 18-year-old participant in the study recollected,

> We were drinking at a party, and I sat down on a couch in another room to chill out and gather myself, when this girl that I knew and I could tell had had a few too many had thrown herself upon me. I realized that both of us were too messed up to fully comprehend what we were doing, but then she began to reach in my pants and grab my penis.

Group memberships such as being part of Greek fraternities and athletic teams have also been associated with elevated risks of sexual assault. Data from Online College Social Life Survey indicated that heterosexual college men who experienced sexual assault were almost twice as likely to be in a fraternity compared heterosexual men who did not experience sexual assault (Ford & Soto-Marquez, 2016). In a similar vein, Tewksbury and Mustaine (2001) found that male college athletes had twice the odds of being sexually assaulted compared to non-athletes. Some scholars are convinced that the greater risk of sexual victimization among college men who belong to all-male groups is related to the standards of hypermasculinity that these group preserve (Murnen & Kohlman, 2007). Hypermasculine values promote male dominance through sexual aggression on women and orient men to view sex with women as conquests. Therefore, men who subscribe to these values may find it emasculating to report that they were sexually coerced by women fearing their acceptance of being assaulted will threaten their masculinity. This perceived shame results in college men giving into sexual coercion of women, or worse it keeps them from reporting sexual assault altogether.

POSITIVE OUTCOMES OF HOOKING UP

Greater risk of STI contraction, unplanned pregnancies, and sexual assault have siloed researchers into focusing on just the negative outcomes of hooking up. However, over the past few years, researchers have acknowledged the positive aspects of hookups such as the experience of sexual satisfaction. A survey of 4,000 college students found that more than 80% of college men and women reported enjoying their sexual activity during hookups (England et al., 2008). Owen and Fincham's (2011) study provided support to this finding as college students largely reported positive reactions (such as happy, pleased, excited) than negative reactions (such as empty, awkward, disappointed) to their hookups.

Role of Orgasms in Positive Reactions to Hookups

Owen and Fincham (2011) also found that college men reported more positive and less negative emotional reactions compared to college women. Researchers have attributed the gender disparity in positive reactions to the persistent orgasm gap that exists between men and women—during sexual encounters, men are more likely to experience orgasms than women. According to a nationally representative survey hosted by NBC News, as many as 95% of heterosexual men reported experiencing an orgasm when being sexually intimate with their partners (Frederick et al., 2018). In comparison, only 65% of heterosexual women reported experiencing an orgasm during similar sexual encounters. Piemonte and associates (2019) provided empirical evidence to the claim that orgasms mediate the relationship between gender and positive emotional responses to hookups. In other words, orgasming during hookups increased the intensity of feeling happy, excited, proud, and confident. Since men were more likely to experience orgasms, they were also more likely to experience these positive feelings compared to women.

Even though women are less likely to experience orgasms, they are more likely to fake orgasms. According to a study published in *Archives of Sexual Behavior*, 58.8% of females reported pretending an orgasm during sex (Herbenick et al., 2019). The prevalence of women faking orgasm does not negate the possibility of men faking orgasms too. Seguin and Milhausen (2016) found that men faked an orgasm in 29% of their sexual encounters. They were most likely to fake orgasms during penile-vaginal intercourse and during oral sex.

The association between faking orgasms and sexual pleasure is not as straightforward as the association between genuine orgasms and sexual pleasure. This is because people have different motives to fake orgasms, and some of these motives are associated with positive sexual experiences while others are not. People fake orgasms (a) out of concern for their partners' feelings, (b) to enhance the quality of partners' sexual experience, (c) out of fear of their own sexual inadequacy, (d) to arouse themselves to a point where they experience a genuine orgasm, and (e) to stop the sex when they are not enjoying themselves (Cooper, Fenigstein, & Fauber, 2014; McCoy, Welling, & Shackelford, 2015). Previous research shows that faking orgasms to heighten sexual arousal are more likely to lead to orgasms and are thus more likely to be tied to positive emotional outcomes compared to faking orgasms to save partners' face (Barnett et al., 2019).

Using orgasms as a sole indicator of sexual satisfaction has garnered criticism on the grounds of taking a male-centered and medicalized view of sex. Studies have shown that when it comes to women's sexual satisfaction, it is much broader than just experiencing orgasms; sometimes sexual pleasure may not include orgasms at all. As one female participant in Nicolson and Burr's (2003) study investigating female sexual satisfaction insisted,

> Kissing is very important for me and touching is very important. Not sex as such, all this because for me it is affection [sic]. For me, I love touch. For me, kissing it almost gives the same pleasure like having real sex. So, yes with the man with whom I was involved that was a very important part for me. (p. 1739)

Researchers have responded to this critique by accounting for other factors that have been associated with sexual pleasure and satisfaction. For instance, Snapp et al. (2015) measured participants' sexual satisfaction from hookups based on these four statements: "It was a good experience," "It made me happy," "I liked how my body felt," and "It made me feel closer to the other person." This allowed Snapp et al. (2015) to accurately measure sexual satisfaction by factoring in physical self-esteem, emotional intimacy, and emotional affect, and not just rely on one single predictor—orgasms.

CURRENT STUDY

In this study, I examined the occurrence of risky sexual behaviors and sexual assault during hookups, and assessed the sexual pleasure and guilt experienced by students after hooking up. Furthermore, I looked at the effect of gender and meeting contexts on these hookup outcomes to answer the following questions:

• Are men more likely to engage in riskier sexual behaviors compared to women?
• Are women more likely to experience sexual assault during hookups?
• Are some meeting contexts riskier than others?
• Do men and women differ in their experiences of sexual satisfaction and regret?

Risky Sexual Behaviors

To examine students' engagement in risky sexual behaviors, I asked them to identify all the sexual behaviors they had engaged in during their most recent hookup. The list included kissing and genital touching (colloquially called "making out"), oral sex, vaginal sex, and anal sex. For oral, vaginal, and anal sex, students were asked if they used a condom or any type of protection or contraceptives.

To rank order the riskiness of sexual behaviors—from least risk of contracting STI to the most risk of contracting STI—I dichotomized the hookups as penetrative hookups or non-penetrative hookups based on the sexual behaviors that had the highest degree of physicality. Hence, hookups that included only kissing and/or genital touching were coded as non-penetrative hookups. In comparison, hookups that involved oral, vaginal, and/or anal sex (with or without kissing and/or genital touching) were coded as penetrative hookups. Second, participants who engaged in penetrative hookups using protection were coded as protected penetrative hookups and participants who engaged in penetrative hookups without protection were coded as unprotected penetrative hookups.

According to previous research, students' level of intoxication, familiarity with hookup partners, and feelings (romantic and sexual) toward their hookup partners affect their likelihood of engaging in risky sexual behaviors during hookups. With that in mind, I asked students to report the following factors:

Alcohol Consumption and Drug Use

Students also reported their alcohol consumption (1 = none at all to 5 = a great deal) and if they had used drugs (yes or no) before or during the hookup.

Familiarity with Hookup Partners

To measure familiarity with hookup partners, I asked participants how frequently they communicated with their hookup partners (1 = we met that day/night, to 5 = daily) and how frequently they hooked up with their partners (1 = only that one time to 9 = more than once a day).

Feelings toward Hookup Partners

To measure feelings toward hookup partners, I asked participants if they were interested in pursuing as romantic relationship with their hookup partners (1 = not at all interested to 4 = very interested). Along with romantic interest in hookup partners, I also asked participants how sexually attracted they were to their hookup partners (5 = very attracted to 1 = not at all attracted) and if they were interested in pursuing a romantic relationship with their hookup partners (1 = not at all interested to 4 = very interested).

Are Men More Likely to Engage in Riskier Sexual Behaviors Compared to Women?

Results showed that both male and female college students engaged in different sexual behaviors in varying degrees during their last hookup. Among males, vaginal or anal sex was the most frequent, making out was the least frequent. Among females, making out was the most frequent, and the least frequent was vaginal or anal sex. More male students compared to female students reported using condoms or other means of protection during their last hookup. These results suggest that male college students have a higher proclivity to engage in riskier sexual behaviors than female college students, but they are also more likely to practice safe sex than female college students.

Students reported low to medium levels of alcohol consumption, and only 20% of students reported using drugs before or during their most recent hookup. There were no gender differences in alcohol consumption, but there were gender differences in drug use—27% of college men compared to only 14% of college women used drugs during their most recent hookups.

Table 5.1 Percentage of Male and Female Students Participating in Various Sexual Activities during Their Most Recent Hookup

	Male in % (N = 140)	Female in % (N = 178)
Making Out (Kissing & Genital Touching)	41	59
Oral Sex	45	55
Vaginal Sex or Anal Sex	46.3	54
Condom Use / Protection	64	52

There were also no gender differences in the level of familiarity with and feelings toward hookup partners. On average, students communicated with their partner on a weekly to a monthly basis, had hooked up with them between once a month and every two to three months, and had a medium to high romantic interest toward their hookup partners.

I ran a multinomial logistic regression to see which of the above factors predicted students' likelihood of engaging in risky sexual behaviors. For male college students, only two factors emerged significant: drug use and alcohol consumption during hookups. Drug use during hookups increased their odds of risky sexual behaviors, whereas alcohol consumption diminished these odds. Students who consumed more alcohol were found to be more likely to make out (i.e., stick to sexual behaviors of lower physicality) compared to having protected penetrative sex.

Results for female college students were different. Contrary to their male counterparts, drug use decreased female students' odds of engaging in risky sex. Another factor that reduced their odds of risky sex was familiarity with their hookup partners—students who hooked up with their hookup partners more frequently were more likely to just make out instead of having sex with them (unprotected or unprotected). The only factor that increased female students' likelihood of engaging in risky sexual behaviors is their sexual attraction toward their hookup partners.

Are Women More Likely to Experience Sexual Assault During Hookups?

Similar to Online College Social Life Survey, I measured sexual assault using six questions whether (a) their hookup partners touched them sexually without their consent; (b) their hookup partners tried to physically force them to have sexual intercourse, but they got out of the situation without having intercourse; (c) their hookup partners had intercourse with them that they did not want to when they were incapacitated; (d) they had hooked up with their partners even when they didn't want to, (e) they had performed oral sex or hand stimulation of their hookup partners because they did not want to have intercourse, but felt they should give them an orgasm, and (f) they touched their hookup partners sexually without their consent. The first five questions measured sexual victimization, and the last question measured sexual assault perpetration. Students responded in either yes or no.

On average, 85% of students responded not experiencing sexual victimization and 90% responded not sexually assaulting their partners' sexual assault perpetration. However, there were significant gender differences in reports of sexual assault.

Contrary to previous research, a higher percentage of male students reported sexual assault on all counts compared to female college students, and these differences were statistically significant. At the same time, a greater percentage of male compared to female college students also perpetrated sexual assault.

Consistent with previous studies, alcohol consumption, drug use, and group memberships were shown to affect students' likelihood of experiencing and perpetrating sexual assault. College men who used drugs during or before their hookups were more likely to experience sexual assault and more likely to sexually assault their partners. Alcohol consumption also showed similar effects except for increasing students' odds of reluctantly offering oral sex to avoid intercourse. Results also showed that male students who belonged to

Table 5.2 Percentage of Male and Female Students Reporting Sexual Assault Victimization and Sexual Assault Perpetration during Their Most Recent Hookup

Sexual Assault Indicators	Male Students (%)	Female Students (%)
Did your hookup partner touch you sexually without your consent?	24	11
Did your hookup partner you hooked up with try to physically force you to have sexual intercourse, but you got out of the situation without having intercourse?	19	5
Did your hookup partner you hooked up with have sexual intercourse with you that you did not want when you were drunk, passed out, asleep, drugged, or otherwise incapacitated?	16	5
Did you hook up with your hookup partner even when you didn't want to?	21	7
Did you perform oral sex or hand stimulation of your hookup partner you hooked up with because you did not want to have intercourse, but felt you should give them an orgasm?	21	8
Did you touch your hookup partner sexually without his/her/their consent?	16	4

Greek fraternities and athletic teams were more likely to experience and commit sexual assault compared to students who did not belong to these groups.

Similar to college men, alcohol consumption was also related to college women's reports of sexual victimization and sexual assault. However, college women differed from college men in terms of drug use and its effect on sexual assault. College women who used drugs before or during their hookups were more likely to reluctantly hook up with partners and be sexually assaulted in an incapacitated state. Being members of athletic teams and sororities was also found to be unrelated to sexual victimization and sexual assault perpetration.

Are Some Meeting Contexts Riskier than Others?

To examine if certain meeting contexts are riskier than others, I examined how the following factors differed across the four meeting contexts (party, school, dating apps, and work): type of risky sexual behaviors students engaged in, alcohol consumption, drug use, and reports of sexual victimization and perpetration for both male and female college students.

Results showed that both male and female college students who met their hookup partners at parties and in school were the most likely to make out or engage in protected penetrative sex and the least likely to engage in unprotected penetrative sex. In contrast, students who met their hookup partners through online dating apps were also most likely to engage in protected or unprotected penetrative sex. As many as 36% of college men and 27% of college women who met their hookup partners through dating apps reported having unprotected sex during their most recent hookup. Most of the male college students who met their hookup partners at work reported making out with them, and an equal percentage engaged in either protected penetrative or unprotected penetrative sex. In comparison, a small percentage of female college students engaged in unprotected penetrative sex with their hookup partners from work, and a majority of them limited their hookup behaviors to just making out. These results show that dating app as a meeting context is most likely related to risky sexual behaviors followed by school, parties, and work.

In terms of alcohol consumption and drug use, college men who met their hookup partners at school had the highest level of intoxication followed by students who met their partners at work and in parties. Among college women, this trend was slightly different—the highest level of intoxication was reported by women who met their hookup partners at parties followed by those who met their partners at work and in school. For both men and women, the level of intoxication was lowest when hooking up with someone they met on dating apps. Drug use was the most frequent among college men who met their partners at school followed by work and dating apps. They were least likely to use drugs with partners whom they had met at parties. No such difference in drug use across meeting contexts was noticed among college women.

Lastly, reports of sexual assault victimization and sexual assault perpetration varied by meeting context, but only for male college students. 82% of college men who reported experiencing sexual assault during hookups met their hookup partners through school. Hooking up with someone from work or through dating apps were the second and third most likely instances of experiencing and perpetrating sexual assault. When hooking up with someone they met at parties, none of the college men reported attempts of forced sex, incapacitated sex, and non-consensually touching their hookup partners, and only 3% to 7% of college men reported unwanted sexual contact, reluctantly hooking up, and reluctantly performing oral sex to avoid intercourse.

Do Men and Women Differ in Their Experiences of Sexual Satisfaction and Regret?

In this study, I measured students' sexual satisfaction as an indicator of their positive emotions, and sexual regret as an indicator of negative emotions. I used Snapp et al.'s (2015) scale as a measure of students' sexual satisfaction. Based on this scale, I asked students to record students' level of agreement (1 = strongly disagree to 5 = strongly agree) to the following five statements as it pertained to their most recent hookup: *It was a good experience, I enjoyed the sexual activity, It made me happy, I like how my body felt, and It made me feel closer to the person.* In addition to these five factors, lastly, I also asked students to report their agreement to the statement, "I regret hooking up with my hookup partner."

Results showed that, on average, both male and female college students reported high sexual satisfaction and medium to low sexual regret. Furthermore, male and female college students' sexual satisfaction and sexual regret were not significantly different.

Next, I examined factors that predicted students' sexual satisfaction and regret. I ran two separate hierarchical multiple regression analyses, one for each sexual outcome variable. Both the analyses included five sets of predictor variables that have been associated with sexual satisfaction and regret during hookups. They were (a) familiarity with hookup partners, (b) feelings toward hookup partners (romantic and sexual), (c) event-level factors (alcohol and drug use during or before hookup, type of sexual behaviors engaged in during hookup (making out, protected penetrative sex, unprotected penetrative sex), (d) occurrence of sexual assault and unwanted hookups, and (e) experience of orgasm (had an orgasm or faked an orgasm), and (f) students' attitudes toward sex. I used Hendrick et al.'s (2006) scale to measure students' sexual attitudes. Some examples of these items were "I do not need to be committed to a person to have sex with him/her," and "casual sex is acceptable." Students' age, sexual orientation, race, and meeting contexts were held as controls in this analysis.

Male Students' Sexual Satisfaction and Regret

For male college students, the following factors increased their sexual satisfaction in hookups: (a) a higher degree of sexual attraction and romantic interest in their hookup partners, (b) use of drugs before or during their hookups, and (c) penetrative (both protected and unprotected) compared to non-penetrative hookups. In terms of sexual regret, male students who were not sexually attracted to their partners reported more regret compared to male students who were sexually attracted to their partners.

Female Students' Sexual Satisfaction and Regret

For female college students, the following factors increased their sexual satisfaction in hookups: (a) a higher degree of sexual attraction and romantic interest toward hookup partners, (b) greater familiarity with hookup partners, (c) experiencing orgasm, (d) not using drugs before or during hookups, (e) having protected penetrative sex, and (f) having sexually permissive attitudes. Results also showed that female college students who reported their last hookup being undesired (i.e., they had hooked up even when they did not want to) were five times less likely to report sexual satisfaction compared to students who hooked up willingly. In terms of sexual regret, female students (a) who hooked up less frequently with their partners, (b) who only made out compared to protected penetrative sex, and (c) who engaged in unwanted hookups reported higher sexual regret. Among the control variables, age and meeting contexts emerged as significant predictors. Older college students compared to younger ones and who had met their hookup partners at parties compared to dating apps reported greater sexual pleasure.

IMPLICATIONS OF RESULTS ON CURRENT HOOKUP CULTURE

In this section of the study, I aimed to account for the positive and negative physical and emotional outcomes of hooking up. Negative outcomes were assessed in terms of students' engagement in risky sexual behaviors, their experiences of sexual assault, and their feelings of sexual regret. Positive outcomes were assessed in terms of their experience of orgasms and sexual satisfaction. I also intended to find if these positive and negative outcomes differed by gender or meeting context. I accomplished this goal by examining (a) if college men were more likely to engage in risky sexual behaviors than college women, (b) if college women were more likely to experience more sexual assault than men, (c) if some meeting contexts were riskier than others, and (d) if college women and men differed in their experiences of sexual satisfaction and regret.

According to the findings, approximately 42% of students had hookups involving non-penetrative sexual acts such as kissing and/or genital touching, and 59% of students had hookups involving sexual intercourse (oral, vaginal, and/or anal sex). Among the students who had sexual intercourse, 31% reported not using any protection. Results showed that, compared to college women, college men engaged in higher physicality sexual behaviors (protected and unprotected penetrative sex compared to kissing or genital touching). But college men were also more likely to practice safe sex compared to college women. The lack of use of protection among females can be seen as a lack of women's assertiveness and agency in negotiating condom use in the context of heterosexual coupling.

Drug use increased college men's odds of engaging in risky sexual behaviors, but alcohol use decreased those odds. This dampening effect of alcohol consumption on college men's willingness to engage in riskier sexual behaviors can be explained when we factor in two things: (a) average level of intoxication and (b) the overall condom use among college men. First, college men reported moderate to low level of drinking. Second, results showed that 80% of college men who engaged in penetrative sex used protection. Thus, the level intoxication was not enough to impair their ability to process safety cues, and their overall awareness of safe sex practices may have reduced their chances of engaging in risky sex.

Alcohol consumption did not affect college women's chances of risky sexual behaviors. Drug use had an opposite effect on college women compared to college men as it decreased their odds of engaging in risky sexual behaviors. Another factor that reduced college women's odds of engaging in risky sexual behaviors is the frequency with which they hooked up with their partners. This lends support to previous research's claim that familiarity engenders trust and comfort between hookup partners, which allows them to negotiate condom and contraceptive use with more ease.

In terms of sexual assault, an optimistic finding of the study was the infrequent occurrence of sexual assault among college women. Less than 10% of college women reported being coerced into sex or being assaulted in an incapacitated state. This percentage is lower than extant literature, which puts the total percentage of college women experiencing sexual assault between 20% and 25%. This reduction in the cases of female sexual victimization can be attributed to stricter campus policies and social movements like #MeToo and #Timesup that provide necessary support to college women to report cases of sexual assault and hold perpetrators accountable.

Reports of male sexual victimization stood in sharp contrast to female sexual victimization—close to 20%, that is, one in five college men reported being sexually assaulted. The sexual assaults ranged from unsolicited sexual touch to sexual coercion. Post hoc analyses showed that these sexual victimizations occurred in heterosexual coupling with the sexual assault perpetrators being female. Considering these results, I insist that educational institutes raise awareness about sexual assault experienced by college men. With the near absence of male sexual victimization in scholarly work, popular press, and college policies, it is easy to assume that sexual assault does not affect men. The cultural conversation today has attuned women to understand the importance of being asked for consent, especially in heterosexual sexual encounters. In the same way, we must take steps to normalize and encourage men demanding consent from their partners, be it in same-sex or opposite-sex coupling.

When gauging the riskiness of meeting context, I considered two factors: the riskiness of sexual behaviors and the odds of experiencing sexual assault in those meeting contexts. According to the findings, both college men and women had the highest chances of having risky sex with partners they met through dating apps. Among the 58 students who reported having unprotected sex, more than half of them (55%) met their hookup partners on dating apps. Previous studies have identified alcohol consumption, familiarity with, and romantic intentions toward hookup partners as reasons that contribute to the lack of using protection during sex. Contrary to previous research, students who met their partners through dating apps reported the lowest level of alcohol consumption. This suggests that students' willingness to engage in risky sex could not be attributed to them being incapacitated by alcohol. This result also lends support to scholars who have argued that students' condom use will be low when hooking up with people they are less familiar with compared to people they know such as friends and ex-partners.

With regard to sexual assault, school was the riskiest meeting context for college men. A disproportionate number of these sexual assault cases happened when college men hooked up with someone they met at school. There are two ways to explain this result: level of inebriation and institutional trust. One of the main reasons why parties have been cited as the most likely context for college men to experience sexual assault is because parties are always associated with heavy drinking. Thus, the assumption is that college men who attend parties get heavily inebriated which, in turn, makes them more susceptible to sexual assault. In this study, the highest level of inebriation was found among college students who met their hookup partners in school settings.

This shows that it is not so much the meeting context but the level of intoxication that affects' male college students' probability of sexual victimization.

When discussing the role that interpersonal trust plays in hookup behaviors among college students, Kuperberg and Padgett (2015) discussed the concept of *institutionalized trust*. The researchers defined institutional trust as trust that people have in each other because of being affiliated to the same institutions such as churches and schools. The researchers argued that when students hook up with others with whom they have high institutional trust, they perceive those hookups come with "a degree of safety and mitigation of risks," which makes them more likely to engage in riskier sexual behaviors. This study shows that the institutional trust could increase the risk of sexual assault.

In terms of positive and negative emotional reactions to hookups, I identified factors that are both common and unique to college men and women that determine their sexual satisfaction and sexual regret. Findings showed that the orgasm gap is still persistent as almost twice the number of college men than college women (63% vs. 37%) experienced orgasm in their last hookup encounter. However, experiencing orgasms did not significantly determine sexual satisfaction among men. Other factors such as engaging in penetrative versus non-penetrative sex and being sexually and romantically attracted to their partners enhanced their sexual satisfaction. While previous research has shown that increased physicality and sexual and/or physical attraction are important to men, common knowledge seems to dictate that men covet emotional distance from their short-term sexual partners. The result from the current study challenges this inherently gender-specific narrative by showing the important role that both physical and emotional intimacy play in men's sexual satisfaction.

On the flip side, even though fewer college women reported experiencing orgasms, they played a significant role in determining their sexual satisfaction. This result suggests that while orgasms are not the only source of sexual satisfaction, they still play a significant role in determining their sexual satisfaction. Like college men, college women's sexual satisfaction was also enhanced by their degree of romantic and sexual attraction toward their hookup partners. Unlike men, the type of sexual behaviors they engaged in did not affect their sexual pleasure, but it did affect their sexual regret. College women who engaged in only kissing and/or genital touching experienced more regret than college women who engaged in protected oral, vaginal, or anal sex. This is an instance where one experiences regret not because of something that one has done, rather for something one has not done.

Another trend that I noticed in college women's emotional reactions to hookups is the level of agency they had in the hookup process. When college women engaged in unwanted hookups, had unprotected sex, and were under the influence of drugs, they either reported more sexual satisfaction or more sexual regret. This finding adds nuance to the existing conversation in hookup literature that portrays women to be uniquely disadvantaged by hookups. It is not college women's participation in or abstention from hookups; rather, it is more the agency they have during the hookup process that affects their well-being.

MAIN TAKEAWAYS

- Students report kissing, genital touching, and protected and unprotected penetrative sex during hookups; most students practice safe sex.
- Students are reporting low alcohol and drug use during hookups; drug use affects college men and women differently.
- Hookups with partners met on dating apps have a higher chance of sexual escalation compared to other meeting contexts.
- Less than 10% of college women reported any form of sexual assault or coercion. In comparison, 20% of college men (i.e., one in every four) reported being sexually assaulted.
- Male sexual assault cases were the most common in school meeting contexts. High levels of alcohol consumption and familiarity with partners may have contributed to the assaults.
- Physical and emotional intimacies are central to male sexual pleasure.
- Refraining from higher-order sexual behaviors and lack of sexual agency contribute to college women's feelings of sexual regret.

Chapter 6

Sugar Dating

An Alternate Route to Casual Sex

Nowadays, college students' foray into the realm of short-term non-committal sexual relations is not only through hookups; alternate routes such as sugar dating have made it possible for college students to experiment with such transient sexual companionships without any relational commitment. Sugar dating, colloquially called *sugaring*, is compensated dating facilitated through online platforms such as *Seeking Arrangement* and *Whats Your Price*. Compensated dating is defined as "a date-like meeting . . . where a middle-aged man and a school-aged girl spend time together, followed by sex and then the man's provision of money or gifts to the girl" (Song & Morash, 2016, p. 67). To put it bluntly, in compensated dating, older men pay young girls to have sex with them. Apart from sex, these school-aged girls are also expected to engage in sexually charged interactions with their older male clients and provide them with the "girlfriend experience." This means that young girls are expected to spend time with their older male clients by going on vacations, restaurants, and movies, and engage in other activities that simulate the same level of intimacy found in traditional relationships (Monto & Morad, 2020). Despite the artificiality of this intimacy, both parties buy into this *myth of mutuality* whereby the school-aged girls and their older clients both suspend the belief that the relationship is transactional and instead pretend that there is an organic, emotional investment from both parties.

Compensated dating was originally prevalent in sub-Saharan countries, but it has also started gaining massive popularity in the Western world because of *sugaring* sites such as *Seeking Arrangement*, *Whats Your Price*, and *Secret Benefits*. Sugaring shares some similarities with the traditional form of compensated dating, but it also has some distinguishing characteristics. Similar to compensated dating, a traditional sugaring relationship involves older wealthy men called *sugar daddies*, who are looking for attractive younger college-aged females, called *sugar babies.* The relationship terms established between the sugar daddy and the sugar baby is called an *arrangement* or a *deal.* These arrangements and deals are either written or verbal contracts where both the sugar daddy and the sugar baby clarify their expectations (Motyl, 2013). Even though sugar daddies do not always expect sugar babies to have sexual intercourse with them, they do expect some form of sexual and emotional gratification from them. These demands may include sexting, fellatio, and simulating a girlfriend experience. In return, sugar babies expect to be monetarily compensated in cash, wire transfers, or through gifts. Sugar babies and daddies also negotiate other details such as frequency of interaction, type of interaction, and ways and frequency of getting paid.

Unlike traditional compensated dating, in sugar dating the monetary benefactors may also be older wealthy women called *sugar mommas.* In the same vein, sugar babies are not always female; male students also report participating in sugar dating. The website *Whats Your Price* uses gender-neutral terms such as "generous members" instead of using sugar daddies/mommas and "beautiful members" instead of sugar babies.

Sugar dating websites also refrain from promoting themselves as a purely transactional space where older and richer men and women can simply seek out young people for sexual favors in exchange for money. Instead, these websites appeal to people's need for freedom of choice and value optimization. The tagline of *Seeking Arrangement* (now rebranded as just *Seeking*) reads, "Seeking.com is the leading dating site where over 10+ million members find relationships on their terms." By using phrases such as "relationship on their own terms," these websites position themselves as platforms that empower men and women to break the societal shackles and negotiate their own rules of dating. *Secret Benefits* also uses a similar appeal, "Enjoy a new kind of relationship with the partner you deserve." *Whats Your Price* takes a different approach and appeals to people's rationality by stating that *Whats Your Price* allows its members to discover "high quality, frequent first dates" without wasting time. The website also promises its members the safest, easiest, and the most rewarding dating experience.

There are two themes that are common across these sugaring websites. First is the use of aspirational terms to describe sugar mommas and daddies, sugar babies, and sugar relationships. Sugar mommas and daddies are not just older individuals who are willing to pay money to younger individuals. Instead, they are "successful men and women who know what they want," "money is not an issue for them," and are "generous." On the other hand, sugar babies are not just individuals who are willing to barter their bodies for money; they are "attractive people looking for finer things in life." Finally, the sugar relationship is not just transactional, but it is a new form of relationship where partners have the freedom to be direct, open, and brutally honest with each other. The second theme is the use of euphemisms for the monetary transaction that takes place between the sugar daddies or mommas and sugar babies. There is a concerted attempt to veil the payment of money as "generosity" and the acceptance of payment as "accept the bid," "getting reimbursed," "getting an allowance," or "being pampered." Through these advertising strategies, sugaring websites try to distance themselves from the notorious reputation they have earned as being promoters of escort services and prostitution.

IS SUGAR DATING PROMOTING PROSTITUTION?

The stark similarity between sugaring and prostitution—payment of money in exchange for sexually gratifying services—begs the question: *Is sugaring just sugar-coating prostitution?*

To answer this question, Miller (2011) drew parallels between prostitution and sugar dating. Miller (2011) is convinced that sugar babies are "craigslist equivalent to streetwalkers" and websites that facilitate such sugar relationships are "virtual pimps." James Madison University professor Tammy Castle, who analyzes escort websites, supported Miller's position. In an interview with *The Atlantic*, Castle insisted,

> [The administrators of the Seeking Arrangement] are trying to avoid the negative stigma of prostitution by advertising this as just another dating website, but money is exchanged for arrangements that may include sex. (Kitchener, 2014)

Motyl (2013) demonstrated how sugar dating websites cleverly maneuver the grey areas of governmental policies to avoid being convicted for prostitution. She began by clarifying Model Penal Code's (MPC) distinction between what is and what is not considered prostitution. According to MPC, if someone engages in sexual activity as a business, then it is considered prostitution. If, however, sex happens within the context of a relationship or if it happens in conjunction with other activities such as going to dinner or a movie, then it is not considered prostitution. This is often the first point of rebuttal against the claim that sugaring is prostitution. Proponents of sugaring argue that, unlike prostitution, sugaring does not *always* involve sex. The allowance that sugar daddies or sugar mommas pay their sugar babies, in the form of cash or other gifts, does not always hinge on sugar babies performing sexual acts. Instead, sugar babies are paid to provide their sugar daddies and mommas with a fabricated girlfriend or boyfriend experience. As for sugar relationships that do involve sex, it happens as a part of a natural progression that is evident in any other form of romantic relationship.

Nevertheless, there are certain versions of sugar relationships that are more likely to be categorized as prostitution compared to others. Based on the nature of *arrangement*, Scull (2020) identified seven types of sugar relationships. One of the variants of sugar relationships, which Scull (2020) labeled as *sugar prostitution*, has the highest chance of being deemed as sex work. This variant of sugaring relationship involves the exchange of sex for money without any social companionship. To add to that, sugar babies involved in sugar prostitution get paid on a per-meeting basis. In comparison to sugar prostitution, the other six variants of sugar relationships (compensated dating, Compensated Companionship, Sugar Dating, Sugar Friendships, Sugar Friendships with Sexual Benefits, Pragmatic Love) involve higher degrees of companionships. These sugar relationships tend to emulate traditional companionships where sugar babies get paid in luxurious gifts, akin to how people would pamper their partners out of love, and sex happens as a part of the intimacy building process. Scull (2020) also clarified that even though there were no expectations of sexual interactions in these variants of sugar dating, sugar babies usually ended up performing sexual acts for their benefactors.

Lastly, Motyl (2013) mentioned how Section 230 of the Communication Decency Act allows sugaring websites and apps to expunge themselves from claims of facilitating prostitution. According to Section 230, the creators of websites cannot be held accountable for the content that their website users create. This means that even if registered users hint or blatantly offer sex for money, the website creators cannot be liable so long as the websites themselves are not actively involved in the money exchange process or promoting sex. This immunity warranted to sugaring providers was partially curtailed with the introduction of Fight Online Sex Traffic Act (FOSTA) and Stop Enabling Sex Traffickers Act (SESTA) that were signed into law in 2018. Under these laws sugaring websites need to prove that they are taking significant measures to prevent prostitution, solicitation, and sex trafficking. This has forced websites such as *Whats Your Price* to include phrases such as "WhatsYourPrice.com is strictly an online dating website. Escorts are not welcome." In conclusion, sugaring may not be considered prostitution by law, but it is paving the way to prostitution for impressionable young adults.

ARE COLLEGE STUDENTS SUGARING?

The infographics included in the press kit of Seeking Arrangement convinces us that sugar dating is a popular practice among college students. The website claims as many as 3 million American college students have registered as sugar babies and that their membership grows at the rate of 7% per year. The website also includes the *Top 20 Sugar Baby Universities* in the United

States. In 2020, they also compiled a list of *Top 10 Community College Sugar Babies*. Arizona State University (ASU) is the top-ranking university with 2,742 registered sugar babies, followed by Indiana University (IU) and New York University (NYU) each accounting for 1,540 and 1,507 sugar babies. At first glance, these staggering numbers convince us that sugaring is pervasive among college students. However, when these numbers are considered within the context of the total student population of these academic institutions, we realize that the percentage of students engaging in sugar dating is, in fact, much lower than what Seeking Arrangement convinces us to believe. For instance, the total student population of ASU is 42,529, IU is 32,991, and NYU is 26,339. This means that less than 5% of students in these universities participate in sugaring. The nationally representative sample of students recruited as participants for the current study also showed a similar trend. Out of 318 students, only 46 (14%) reported using sugar dating apps. This shows that a relatively small percentage of students are partaking in this form of compensated dating.

Besides using advertising tactics to promote the dominance of sugaring in college campuses, websites like *Seeking Arrangement* are also notorious for promoting a stereotypical image of sugar babies. As Daly (2017) in her investigation on sugar babies and sugar daddies in Canadian campuses point out, people expect a typical sugar baby to be "white, blonde, girl-next-door." However, the reality often tends to be farther from this image popularized by these websites. In the present study, I found that out of the 46 students who reported sugaring, (a) 20 were male and 26 were female and (b) 21 were White and 26 were racial minorities. Moreover, a higher percentage of LGB compared to heterosexual male college students participated in sugaring. This trend was opposite for female college students. These results provide testimonial to the fact that being a sugar baby is no longer relegated to Caucasian/ White females and that sugaring is gaining prominence among males as well as racial and sexual minorities.

Given this disconnect between the fabricated imagery of sugaring popularized by sugaring websites, and the burgeoning of sugaring on college campuses, albeit slow, it behooves on scholars to investigate this phenomenon and the implications it has on college students.

Why Are College Students Sugaring?

It is true that one of the main motives students have to do sugaring is to make money. But there is a fair amount of variation in how students decide to use this money. The popular belief is that students use the money they make from sugaring to pay off their education loans. When we log into the *Seeking Arrangement* website, the first thing that catches our attention is the

"Current Student Debt Counter" that is placed front and center on the landing page. The website adopts this strategy to impress the debilitating college student debt on its potential customers. As of 2021, the current student debt is at approximately $1,788,677,270,312. Brandon Wade, the CEO of Seeking Arrangement, positions his company as an *economic relief* program that is much more convenient compared to other traditional financial aid programs such as Free Application for Federal Student Aid (FAFSA). Wade has even boasted that *Seeking Arrangement* has helped millions of students avoid debt by providing them with an opportunity to make money while still in college.

Reports from mainstream media and scholarly research have shown that students indeed use sugaring websites to pay off their tuition and education loans. Wexler (2013) did an investigative piece titled *The Secret World of Sugar Babies* for *Cosmopolitan* magazine. Abby, one of the sugar babies Wexler (2013) interviewed, complained, "I pay for school myself and it's been a struggle, so the offers are tempting. I currently have about $30,000 in loans and more to go before graduation." Abby mentioned using her monthly $3,000 allowance from sugaring to pay off her student loans. Taylor, another student at Hunter College in New York City, recalled being directed to a sugaring website after searching for terms such as "tuition," "debt," and "money for school." While creating a profile in one of the sugaring websites, Taylor mentioned putting in the requirement that sugar daddies would have to pay her an allowance of $1,000 to $3,000 a month; she would reject the solicitations from sugar daddies who did not have the financial ability to pay the specified amount. Results of the current study also showed that 16 of the 46 students reported sugaring to pay off student loans and other school expenses.

Besides loans and tuition, college students have other expenses they need to take care of, such as rent, food, and commute. In 2013, *Citi and Seventeen* magazine conducted the *College Student Pulse* national survey of more than 1,000 college students. According to their findings, four out of five college students take up part-time jobs along with attending college full-time to pay for these expenses. Usually, students put in long hours in these jobs for minimal pay. Sugaring provides students with a convenient alternative for making money because (a) sugaring typically pays more money and (b) sugaring requires lesser time commitment compared to these minimum wage jobs. In the present study, 21 of the 46 students who reported getting paid through sugaring made an average of $1,750 per month. Thus, sugaring provides students with a win-win scenario—they make more money in less time, and they can invest this time toward schoolwork. Despite this benefit of having additional time on hand, results from the current study showed that sugaring was related to inferior scholastic performance. The average GPA of students who did sugaring was 2.76 compared to a 3.22 GPA of students who refrained from sugaring. In addition, 38.2% of students who did sugaring aspired for academic degrees higher than just a bachelor's degree compared to 62% of college students who did not participate in sugaring.

Another finding from the current study contradicted the common assumption that students primarily participate in sugaring to pay off their loans. 50% of students reported using sugaring websites to make money for covering living expenses compared to 35% of students who reported using sugaring for paying off tuition and loans. Furthermore, students who reported sugaring were just as likely to have student loans as students who did not participate in sugaring. This trend can be explained by the results of *College Student Pulse* survey. According to the survey, only about 18% of American college students reported being responsible for paying their own tuition and loans; these expenses were mostly taken care of by their parents or through financial aid and scholarships. In contrast, 31% of students reported being responsible for paying for their housing and 41% for their food. It then makes sense that students are more likely to use their sugaring allowance to offset these living expenses instead of tuition and loans.

Besides living expenses, the *College Student Pulse* survey also showed that 75% of college students reported being responsible for discretionary spending such as clothing and travel. It comes as no surprise that 19 out of the 46 students in the present study cited sugaring to pay for expenses related to eating, drinking, buying clothes, and other luxurious purchases. Students use the money and gifts they receive from their affluent sugar daddies and sugar mommas to experience what Brandon Wade calls the "finer things in life," a privilege that is typically not warranted to "broke" college students. For example, Chou (2017) reported about a female sugar baby who received $20,000 to discuss books on the phone with her sugar daddy; she admitted to buying expensive items such as Louboutin and YSL shoes using her sugaring allowance.

Apart from sugaring to pay off tuition, living, and discretionary expenses, students in the current study cited two other reasons for sugaring. 15% of students reported using sugaring for "being mentored by sugar momma/sugar daddy." This motive is in line with the promotional strategy used by Seeking Arrangement according to which the website gives sugar babies an opportunity to find mentors who offer valuable financial and career advice to students. During a 2014 interview on *The View*, Jenny McCarthy asked Kristen, a 22-year-old sugar baby why she chose to do sugaring to make money when she could be working at Starbucks. Kristen defended her choice by saying, "I am a very entrepreneurial-driven person and I want to find a relationship with someone similar to me." Valentina Casamento, a 26-year-old sugar baby based in New Jersey, who aspired to be a gym owner, justified her decision of sugaring in a similar fashion. In her interview with the *Business Insider*, Casamento emphasized, "He [sugar daddy] will totally help me in all the ways that I need, whether it's financially, emotional support, business advice—all of that" (Lebowitz, 2017).

Lastly, 19% of students in the present study mentioned using sugar dating apps "as a joke." This is in line with the finding from Lenze's (2020) study where she interviewed eight females who participated in sugaring while attending college. Lenze (2020) found that her interviewees often reported that they started sugaring "as a joke." In other words, students started sugaring as a fun activity to engage in along with their friends without any serious intention to follow through. One of Lenze's participants, 19-year-old Marie, recollected,

> My friend had said that she was on there [on seeking.com]. I kind of thought it was a joke. So, she made me an account, but I didn't take it too seriously at the time. And so, I just kind of, like, just shrugged it off, and so, I wasn't really on it at the time. [. . .] I just didn't mess with it because I was like, "what, what are you doing?" And then I was like, "Oh, she actually did that!" So. . . . It was just that casual and brief and then not.

This result calls attention to two important aspects of sugaring among college students. First, like sex work, students are often introduced to sugaring through friends or people in their extended social network. And second, sugaring may often start as an act of amusement but can eventually turn into a serious pursuit. To this end, it is imperative to examine the role peer approval and support plays in promoting and normalizing sugaring among college students. This was beyond the purview of my study, but I encourage future studies to probe into this matter.

What Do Students Do for Their Sugar Daddies and Mommas?

As mentioned earlier, sugar babies are not expected to have sex with their benefactors to get paid. At the same time, sugar daddies and mommas do expect some form of sexual interaction from their sugar babies or expect their sugar babies to provide them with a romantic partner experience. I asked the 46 students who reported using sugar dating to indicate the nature of interaction they had with their latest sugar daddy or momma. This included (a) sexting, (b) hooking up, (c) having sex with their benefactors, and (d) escorting their benefactors to dates, movies, parties, and vacations. Findings showed that out of 46 students, 37% students reported sexting, 35% reported hooking up with, 24% reported having sex with, and 24% reported escorting their sugar daddies and mommas. These results are consistent with the findings from previous research which claim that there is a strong expectation of some form of sexual interaction in sugar relationships that may or may not involve sexual intercourse. Results also showed performing sexual acts increased the odds of getting paid by sugar daddies and mommas. Out of 46 students, 21 reported getting paid by their benefactors. Among these 21 students, 66% reported sexting, 52% reported hooking up, 33% had sex, and 42% escorted their sugar mommas and daddies.

IMPLICATION OF RESULTS ON CURRENT HOOKUP CULTURE

Similar to hooking up, sugaring is also a form of sexual relationship that defies the traditional norms of intimacy and sexuality. My expectation was that students who choose to participate in such a socially deviant form of coupling would differ from students who choose to refrain from it in terms of their attitudes toward sex, dating, and sexual history. Contrary to my expectations, I found that students who participated in sugaring relationships were not more sexually permissive, did not have a greater number of sexual or hookup partners, did not have lower sexual disgust, and did not masturbate or watch porn more frequently compared to students who refrained from sugar dating. In addition, students who participated in sugaring did not have higher dating anxiety compared to non-sugaring counterparts. Readers should interpret these results with caution because of the limited sample size that could have compromised the statistical power of the analyses. I invite future research to investigate a broader range of socio-demographic and psychological correlates that may distinguish students who choose to become sugar babies compared to those who do not. I would also encourage future research to examine if and how participating in sugar dating fundamentally shifts students' understanding and expectations from conventional romantic relationships.

MAIN TAKEAWAYS

- Sugaring is becoming popular among college students; more than 10% of students were sugar babies.
- Students engaged in sugaring mainly to pay for their discretionary expenses.
- A majority of sugar baby students sexted and hooked up with their benefactors, and 3 in 10 of them had sex with their benefactors.
- Sugar dating does not seem to affect students' hookup and sexual behaviors.

Chapter 7

International Students

The Overlooked Student Population in Hookup Literature

As evidenced throughout this book, copious amounts of research have been dedicated to studying US-based college students' hookup behaviors. However, when studying the US college student population, international students have often been excluded, and even when they are included, their responses are lumped together with native-born students (Bonistall, 2020). The cultural coding and social memberships of international students are significantly different than native-born students and should be taken into consideration when documenting their hookup experiences. The handful of studies focused on international students have often considered them as a single homogenous group, when international students hail from several different countries (Hwang, Martirosyan, & Moore, 2016; Kim et al., 2017). This lack of research on a sizeable section of the US college student population, and the reductive treatment of an inherently heterogenous group as a homogenous one, limits the scope of hookup literature. In this final chapter, I address this gap by bringing international students into the fore. First, I provide an overview of the unique challenges international students face during their migration to and tenure in American universities. Following this, I examine their participation in the hookup culture and the impact it has on their sense of belonging.

THE LURE OF AMERICAN HIGHER EDUCATION

Every year, thousands of students from more than 180 countries come to the United States on temporary visas (F1 visa for academic study, M1 for vocational study, and J1 for cultural exchanges) to fulfill their higher education goals. The international student body makes up for a sizable faction of the college population. The Institute of International Education reported that the total number of international students enrolled in US universities in 2018–2019 was 1,095,299 setting an all-time high record (iie.org, 2019). The lion's share of these international students tends to come from Asian countries followed by European and Latin American countries (opendoorsdata.org, 2019).

The United States has been a popular destination for international students because of its high-quality programs, access to more resources, and an education system that is more conducive to learning than what is available in international students' home countries. Additionally, educational degrees earned in the United States have high regard overseas and may lead to better employment prospects. US universities are aware of their global lure in the education sector and invest their time and money in actively recruiting international students (icef.com, 2019). These students are not only a major source of revenue, but they also contribute to the cultural diversity of campus life and enhance the academic community's intellectual prowess. International students pay huge out-of-state tuition fees and bear substantial living costs to earn their degree in the United States.

The United States has reaped the rewards by the influx of international students that go beyond revenue from tuition and campus living. According to a recent report, international students contributed a staggering $57.3 billion to the US economy (Rusu, 2019). Apart from economic gains, international students promote multiculturalism and enhance socialization in US college campuses (Urban & Palmer, 2014). A culturally diverse college campus fosters interaction between domestic and international students, which then leads to the exchange of ideas and information that benefits both parties (Luo & Jamieson-Drake, 2013). Furthermore, international students enrolled in graduate programs also serve as teaching and research assistants satisfying the scholarship and pedagogical needs of their respective departments.

CHALLENGES UNIQUE TO INTERNATIONAL STUDENTS

When transitioning to college life in US universities and colleges, international students face some challenges that are different from their domestic counterparts. Frankly put, the transition from high school to college is turbulent for all students. For many of them, it is the first time they have total agency—students become responsible for living by themselves in dorms or apartments without any parental supervision, keeping up their academic performance without being coddled by their teachers, and being aware of their dietary requirements (which, if not careful, can lead to the infamous "Freshman Fifteen" phenomenon). They are also responsible for building a new social network from scratch, having migrated miles away from their high school friend group.

International students must negotiate all of this as well as figure out the transitional process from a completely different country. This makes their adjustment process more precarious compared to their domestic counterparts. International students need to navigate two major issues when they come to the United States for higher education: the information gap and the cultural gap. First, international students must acquire temporary visas to come to the United States; this process in and of itself can be an uphill climb. After getting their visas and coming to the United States, they need to figure out several things unique to the American way of living. These include getting a social security number, opening a bank account, figuring out employment opportunities (where they can or cannot work based on their immigration status), filing taxes (if they earn money), getting a driver's license, coordinating residential living situations, and even simple day-to-day tasks like getting groceries. They also need to learn about the norms of the US education system such as avoiding plagiarism, scheduling classes, teacher-student correspondence, and navigating online learning management systems. Even after filling up these information gaps, international students must tackle the social and cultural gap between their home country and the United States.

Even though there are over 180 countries represented in the international student body, they are often lumped together as one homogenous group. This homogenous treatment keeps us from acknowledging the wide cultural differences that exist within the international student body. While students from countries such as the Netherlands and Germany may find the United States to be culturally similar to their own, students from countries such as India and China may find themselves worlds apart. Granted, these cultural gaps are shrinking due to globalization and immigration, but there are still some mannerisms and sociocultural codes that international students from certain countries are not privy or accustomed to, which may contribute to a sense of culture shock.

Another factor that affects cultural differences is students' English proficiency. A majority of international students who come to the United States are classified as "non-native speakers" (NNS) of English. Since English is the main language of official and social correspondence in the United States, not being proficient in English impedes the academic adjustment of NNS international students and also acts as a roadblock in socialization with their American peers. For instance, a survey of 454 international students classified as NNS reported not having any close American friends because of the language barrier (Gareis, 2012). Lacking conversational skills in a certain language also causes the lack of cultural knowledge that comes embedded within that language. Therefore, the adjustment and acculturation of NNS international students are not only hindered by the lack of English linguistic proficiency but also the lack of cultural connotations that would have been apparent if they were fluent in American English.

Not all NNS international students struggle with English proficiency. Students from countries where English is commonly used are generally well-versed and conversant. However, another hurdle that NNS international students face is their accents and the social implications those accents carry. While accents from Western countries, such as the UK or Italy, may be perceived as classy, accents from Eastern or otherwise predominantly nonwhite countries, such as China or India, may invite prejudice from US domestic citizens (Stewart, Ryan, & Giles, 1985). Thus, NNS international students often find themselves discouraged and anxious at the thought of fraternizing with their American counterparts, and often form cliques with people from their native countries. Therefore, the acculturation process is the most challenging for students who hail from countries that are both culturally and linguistically different from the United States (Wang et al., 2017).

UNIVERSITY'S ROLE IN
ADDRESSING THESE CHALLENGES

US universities, privy to these academic, linguistic, cultural, and social challenges, provide various forms of support for their international students. For example, universities host orientation programs—typically two- to three-day events organized by offices of international student support—and hold information seminars on a variety of topics that help international students get familiar with American college life. Some of the popular topics covered in these orientation sessions include immigration dos and don'ts, financial aid, medical insurance, scheduling classes, library services, research opportunities, and academic integrity. These orientation programs also include cultural awareness sessions where international students are informed about basic cultural norms of American society. International student orientation sessions also serve as a platform for making social connections for international students as they mingle with other international and local students during information break-out sessions, food breaks, and organized activities. Apart from this initial socialization that is facilitated by the orientation sessions, universities also have buddy systems where international students are paired up with local families and students who act as cultural agents for them.

The overarching motive of these orientation programs is to help international students situate themselves comfortably in their new environment.

However, the way in which international students adjust themselves to this new environment depends on their own individual experiences as explained by Berry's (1997) Bidirectional Model of Acculturation. According to this model, the way in which individuals who have lived in one cultural context tend to live in another cultural context depends on two factors: an individual's identification with their home culture and an individual's identification with the host culture (in this case, American culture). Depending on the variance on both these factors international students can *integrate*, *assimilate*, *separate*, or *alienate*. Integration is the acculturation strategy where international students identify with both their home and host cultures. Assimilation is when international students abandon identification of their home culture completely and choose to identify solely with the host culture. In contrast, separation is when international students completely abandon the host culture and identify solely with their home culture. Finally, alienation is when international students abandon both their home and host cultures.

The outcome of the acculturation process is the sense of belonging that students feel toward campus life. Sense of belonging has been described as the perceived sense of "fitting in" among college students—the extent to which they think they are a part of and feel included in the college community (Strayhorn, 2018). After figuring out their living arrangement and meeting academic demands, the next thing students yearn for is the feeling of fitting in, belonging, or being a part of the college community. Sense of belonging has been of great scholarly interest because it has been shown to be linked to students' academic success, retention, and overall well-being of students (O'Keeffe, 2013).

Research has identified several factors that affect international students' sense of belonging on campus. They include students' living environment, proficiency in English, interaction with professors and peers, and involvement in co-curricular activities. International students who live on campus are shown to have a significantly greater sense of belonging than students who live in off-campus housing. Living in residence halls and creating intimate relationships with other students within a close-knit community foster a markedly greater sense of belonging, especially for international students. Students with lower English proficiency have a lower sense of belonging. Additionally, students who interact with domestic students and locals have a greater sense of belonging. Cultural factors also influence their sense of belonging. Thus, students who come from countries that are culturally congruent with the United States have a higher sense of belonging compared to those who come from culturally distinct countries (for further review, refer to Chaudhuri, 2016).

HOOKING UP FOR ACCULTURATION
AND SEEKING SENSE OF BELONGING

Since hooking up is such a prominent part of the American college experience, I argue that international students will be motivated to hook up to acculturate. Also, international students who participate in hookups while in college—particularly those who have used the acculturation strategies of either integration or assimilation—will have a greater sense of belonging compared to international students who do not hook up.

Literature from organization communication informs us that people's participation in a work culture hinges on a process called *anticipatory socialization*, that is, the process by which people learn about work-life before entering the workforce (Jablin, 2000). Based on this, I argue that international students' anticipatory socialization about the American college life can increase their probability of participating in the dominant college hookup culture. Previous research shows that international students learn about American college life through media portrayals, friends, and family who have been to the United States and their own previous visits to the United States (Postell, 2015).

In the present study, I examined international students' engagement in the American college hookup culture by selecting the responses of students who identified as not being born in the United States. I measured international students' anticipatory socialization by asking them whether they knew about the American college culture and if so where did they learn it from. In addition, I asked them the following questions: (i) their proficiency in conversational English, (ii) length of stay in the United States, (iii) if they had hooked up while they were enrolled in American universities, and if they had, to indicate the nationality of their hookup partners. Their hookup engagement was measured using the same questions as national-born students described in chapters 4 and 5. Lastly, they were asked to report their sense of belonging.

Out of 318 students who completed this survey, only 38 students indicated that they were not born in the United States. Because of this limited sample size, I could not run any statistical analyses to make meaningful comparisons between international students and their American counterparts. Instead, I am presenting descriptive analyses of the international student body that can inform future statistical inquiries with a larger sample size. This analysis also illustrates the importance of accounting for the heterogeneity that exists within the international student body.

International and Naturalized Students:
Similarities and Differences

Out of these 38 students, 16 were on a temporary visa to the United States and 22 were either US citizens or permanent residents. Scholars have defined international students as students who are on temporary visas and are non-native English speakers (Andrade, 2006). Based on this definition, only 16 students qualified as international students in my study. However, I have presented the findings from students who are US citizens or permanent residents (henceforth referred to as "naturalized students") and students on temporary visas (henceforth referred to as "international students"). I have also compared and contrasted the findings between these two groups to show the fair amount of variance that is present within foreign-born students.

For the 16 international students, the median age when they moved to the United States was 18 years and their median current age was 22.5 years. This meant that, on average, international students had spent only four years in the United States. Barring one, all the other students hailed from Latin American, Asian, European, and African countries. Refer table 7.1 for a full list of countries.

Their median GPA was 4.0. There were 10 females and 6 males, and with the exception of two students, the rest identified as straight. In terms of relationship status, nine were single, one was casually dating, and six were in a relationship. These students had an average number of three sexual partners.

For the 22 naturalized students the median age when they moved to the United States was 10.5 years and their current median age was 22 years. This meant that, on average, these students had spent over 10 years in the United States. Similar to international students, a majority of naturalized students also hailed from Latin American, Asian, and African countries. The main difference was that only one naturalized student was from a European country.

Their average GPA was one grade point lower than the students who were on a temporary visa. There were 16 females and 8 males, and with the exception of two students, the rest identified as straight. In terms of relationship status, 17 were single, 2 were casually dating, and 3 were in a relationship. These students also had an average number of three sexual partners.

Past research has shown that English proficiency is an important factor that determined college students' assimilation to American college life and in turn, the hookup culture. 69% of students reported that English was not their native tongue. In spite of this, they reported being very comfortable in having a conversation in English. Their comfort with English as a conversational

Table 7.1 List of Countries of Origin of International Students Who Participated in This Research

Brazil	Vietnam	South Africa	Albania
Peru	Nepal	Egypt	Ireland
Mexico	Indonesia	Angola	Canada
Panama			

Table 7.2   List of Countries of Origin of Naturalized Students Who Participated in This Research

Brazil	China	Ghana	France
Colombia	Philippines	Egypt	
Mexico	Pakistan	Kenya	
Peru	Russia	Angola	
Haiti		Algeria	

language was measured by asking them the question, "How comfortable are you having a conversation in English?" Participants responded on a five-point Likert scale (1 = Not comfortable at all; 5 = Extremely comfortable). The mean score of participants was 4.27. The comfort with conversational English was comparable across naturalized and international students.

I asked the 16 international students where they learned about US culture. 56% said they learned from television and movies, 75% said they learned from social media, 25% said they learned from family who stayed in the United States, 38% learned from their friends who had been to the United States, and 38% learned from their own experience in the United States. On average, students learned about the United States from two to three sources combined. The most popular means of learning about the United States was social media. Based on these results, it would seem that social media has displaced or is currently displacing the role of traditional media as a socialization agent.

Hookup Experiences

Among naturalized students, 20 out of 22 (91%) reported having only 1–5 hookup partners, while 2 (9%) reported having more than 5 hookup partners. Among the 16 international students, the results were slightly different—50% reported having 1–5 hookup partners while the other 50% reported having more than 5 hookup partners.

Among naturalized students, 41% met their hookup partners before coming to their current university, 27% met at university, and 31% had an equal divide. Compared to this, among international students, 75% met most of their hookup partners before university, while 25% met most of their hookup partners at the institution. This shows that international students were initiated or oriented toward the hookup culture from their home countries itself, rather than having their first brush with the hookup culture in the United States. This may be indicative of the global preference for hookups among college students. The hookup culture may have started as an American phenomenon but has evolved to be the default coupling strategy of young adults around the world. These results also show that naturalized students may be more likely to meet their hookup partners at university compared to international students. This can be attributed to naturalized students' longer tenure in the United States. Having been in the United States for more years compared to international students, naturalized students may have gotten more comfortable in navigating the norms of the campus hookup culture. This longer tenure could have also given naturalized students access to a larger preexisting social network (such as friends from high school or hometown who joined the same university) from where they can select their hookup partners. The absence of these preexisting social network for international students may have curtailed their availability of hookup partners.

Only international students were asked to indicate the nationality of their most recent hookup partner. 31% reported that their last hookup partner was American, 69% of them hooked up with someone who was foreign born. In terms of meeting contexts, there were slight differences between international and naturalized students. Out of 16 international students, 25% met at parties, 18% met online, 18% met in class, and 12% met in other locations. Naturalized students had similar meeting context patterns—27% met at parties, 27% met online, 22% met in class, and 9% met in other locations. This shows that parties are the most popular meeting location for both groups of students. In terms of the meeting location hierarchy, naturalized students are more likely to meet their partners in class and through online dating apps compared to international students.

International students and naturalized students were also mostly similar when it came to sexual activities during their most recent hookup. A majority of both international students and naturalized students reported lower-order sexual activities such as kissing and making out. The only difference was that two naturalized students reported participating in anal sex, while none of the international students reported as such. For international students who reported participating in oral or vaginal sex, 60% reported using condoms, while for naturalized students, 63% reported using condoms.

To measure sense of belonging, I asked students to rate the following three statements on a five-point Likert scale: "I feel like I belong here," "I feel like I fit in," and "I am satisfied with my social life on campus" (1 = Strongly Disagree, 5 = Strongly Agree). For both international and naturalized students, the sense of belonging was high (M = 3.69, SD = 0.983). There was also no relation between the total number of hookup partners and the sense of belonging. This means international and naturalized students who had fewer hookup partners had just as much of a sense of belonging to campus as students who had more hookup partners.

IMPLICATIONS OF RESULTS ON
CURRENT HOOKUP CULTURE

Results show that international students are aware of the American college culture and have some hookup experience even before coming to the United States. In terms of Berry's (1997) Bidirectional Model of Acculturation, it seems that international students are both integrating and assimilating into American university culture. They are, in one way or another, identifying with their host culture while adjusting to their new environment. The level of English proficiency is relatively high for international students, which may also be aiding their acclimation to American culture, a part of which is engaging in the college hookup culture. In addition to knowing English, being aware of the American hookup culture through firsthand or second-hand observation helped in understanding some of the culture's nuance. This knowledge is being increasingly conveyed through social media above all other means.

The behaviors of international and naturalized students are mostly similar. This is especially apparent in terms of the number of hookup partners, the number of sexual partners, extent of sexual behaviors during hookups, meeting partners at parties, and condom use. However, the areas that indicate divergence between the two groups are GPA, meeting more of their hookup partners before university, and meeting hookup partners in classes and online. International students reported having higher GPAs than naturalized students, which may indicate a greater scholastic investment. 75% of international students met most of their hookup partners before coming to university, compared to 41% of naturalized students. Another 31% of naturalized students indicated an equal divide between meeting their partners before and at university. The high number of international students meeting a majority of their partners before attending university in the United States further pushes the point that hookups are not exclusively American and is common in other countries too. Even though hookups were common between naturalized and international students, they differed in the location where they met their hookup partners. Naturalized students were more likely to meet their partners in classes and through online dating apps in comparison to international students. This can be attributed to naturalized students being more familiar with norms of academic class culture and online dating culture.

An interesting finding was that international students hooked up more often with non-American students instead of American students. This indicates possible cultural differences or discomfort in hooking up with Americans. Rather than hooking up with someone who is American, international students may feel more comfortable engaging in one of the most prominent aspects of American college life with someone who also has an outsider perspective on the American hookup culture. Engaging in American cultural acts with a fellow partner who has had a similar life experience as one's own—even if both of them are only working with their own perceptions of another culture—may provide some ease into tackling something unfamiliar and exciting.

Lastly, hooking up did not affect students' sense of belonging. This implies that, despite hookups being an integral part of the American college life, engaging in it did not build a sense of belonging. Thus, there may be other factors that contribute to students' sense of belonging such as their engagement in school-based activities, living on campus compared to off campus, and having a strong network of friends in school.

Overall, this chapter illustrates the factors that distinguish foreign-born students (both naturalized and international) that can affect their hookup experiences from students who are born in the United States. Due to the unequal distribution of foreign-born students and US-born students in the sample, it was not possible to compare the hookup experiences of these two groups. Future research can address this issue by oversampling or recruiting a larger pool of international students.

MAIN TAKEAWAYS

- International students have a history of hooking up in their home countries even before coming to the United States.
- Naturalized students and international students are mostly alike despite the difference in the amount of time they have lived in the United States.
- International students mostly hookup with other international students during their tenure in the United States.
- Hooking up (or lack thereof) does not affect international students' sense of belonging.

Conclusion

My goal in this book was to provide readers with an accurate picture of the current hookup culture in American college campuses. A necessary step toward accomplishing this goal was to account for dating apps as a venue for college students to meet hookup partners along with conventional meeting contexts for hookups such as parties, school, and work. College-aged students are one of the most frequent users of dating apps in the United States, and have often reported using these apps for seeking out casual sex partners. A number of studies have even examined the impact of dating apps on the college hookup culture. However, they have not investigated if and how the hookups that ensue from dating apps are fundamentally different from the hookups that ensue from traditional meeting contexts. I addressed this gap within the literature in three steps. First, I compared the sociodemographic and psychological profiles of students who reported meeting a majority of their hookup partners through dating apps compared to other venues. Next, I examined the hookup scripts followed by students who met their most recent hookup partners through a dating app versus at a party, at school, or at work. And finally, I examined the health risks, sexual assault, sexual satisfaction, and sexual regret experienced by students in their most recent hookup, and if these outcomes differed across meeting contexts. I have rehashed some of the main findings from the study below.

Popularity of dating app–initiated hookups. According to this research's findings, dating apps were one of the most popular venues for meeting hookup partners second only to school; a majority of students still reported meeting their hookup partners through school settings (classes, dorms, student clubs, and so on). This result indicates that dating apps are becoming just as popular as parties as venues for meeting hookup partners. Only a small percentage of students reported meeting their partners through work, and this trend was dominant only among older students.

Two main reasons account for the popularity of dating apps as venues for meeting hookup partners: *convenience* and *clarity*. Compared to other avenues, dating apps gave students access to a larger pool of potential hookup partners whom they could get to know and vet using the information provided in their partners' dating profiles. Students also mentioned that hookups solicited through dating apps were more clear and unambiguous compared to hookups solicited at parties, school, or work; in dating-app solicited hookups, students were able to clarify their expectations with their partners online before meeting them face to face. These benefits did not preclude students from having concerns about being *catfished* or physically harmed when hooking up with partners met through dating apps. This lack of trust in dating app–acquainted hookup partners is one of the reasons why students still prefer hooking up with partners met through school. Being affiliated to the same school and having prior familiarity with hookup partners imbibed a greater sense of trust in them compared to partners met through dating apps and at parties.

Profile of students who engage in dating app–initiated hookups. While school and parties were popular for opposite-sex hookups, dating apps were more popular for same-sex hookups. Historically, LGB individuals have relied on online means for meeting sexual partners compared to offline (i.e., face-to-face) venues. Therefore, the current research's finding that a higher percentage of LGB students compared to heterosexual students used dating apps for finding hookup partners is consistent with previous research. Besides sexual orientation, students who primarily used dating apps to meet hookup partners also tended to be more sexually liberal compared to students who met a majority of their hookup partners through school.

Scripts followed during dating app–initiated hookups. Consistent with previous research, results from this study showed that hookup scripts were largely similar to dating scripts. The five hookup script elements that were common across all four meeting contexts (parties, school, dating apps, and work) were *attending event, talking, hanging out, evaluating other*, and *engaging in physical contact*. The script followed by students who hooked up through dating apps was different from the other meeting contexts in two ways: the exclusion of the element *getting to know one another* and the inclusion of the element *discussing plans*. Students who meet their hookup partners through parties, school, and work have to get to know their partners because they usually do not have any information about them prior to meeting them. This situation is different in dating apps because students have prior knowledge about their partners from their partners' dating profiles. Therefore, it is plausible that students who met their hookup partners through dating apps did not explicitly mention this element as a part of their hookup scripts because they already got to know their hookup partners by perusing their dating profiles.

Unlike students who met their hookup partners through other contexts, students who met their hookup partners through dating apps mentioned *discussing plans* as a part of their hookup script. This indicates that in dating app–initiated hookups, students follow what is called a *hybrid hookup script*—a unique script that includes elements from traditional dating scripts while retaining the expectation of casual sex. Similar to dating, students mentioned discussing plans with their hookup partners before meeting them. However, unlike dating, most of these plans centered around having sex.

Physical and emotional outcomes of dating app–initiated hookups. Results showed that students who hooked up with partners using dating apps were the most likely to engage in unprotected penetrative sex despite having the lowest level of intoxication. Dating apps did not lead to higher odds of being sexually assaulted despite students' perceived fear of being harmed by their hookup partners. Feelings of sexual satisfaction and sexual regret also did not significantly vary across meeting contexts. These results show that dating app–initiated hookups may pose a greater threat to students' physical well-being, but they do not detrimental to their emotional well-being any more than hookups initiated through school, parties or work.

Besides exhibiting the nuanced nature of hookups based on the context through which students meet their partners, there were other findings in this research that call to question some of our long-held gender-specific beliefs about the collegiate hookup culture. I have summarized some of those main findings below.

Dissipating gender difference in hookups. Contrary to sexual strategies theory and the sexual double standard theory, the results of this research showed that college women had just as many hookup partners as college men.

Defying gender norms in hookup scripts. Analyses of the hookups scripts showed that college men and women routinely engaged in behaviors that defied gender norms. For example, college men engaged in talking and getting to know their hookup partners, while college women often took the lead in propositioning and making plans for hook ups.

Defying gender norms in sexual outcomes. Some commonly held beliefs about the male hookup experience are that they prefer remaining emotionally detached from their hookup partners and that their sexual satisfaction is solely derived from them experiencing orgasms. Results of the current research challenged these beliefs as orgasms did not predict the likelihood of college men's sexual satisfaction. Instead, the level of physical intimacy and romantic interest toward their partners were the two factors that significantly predicted how sexually satisfied they felt during hookups.

On the other hand, conventional wisdom dictates that women's sexual satisfaction is not affected as much by them experiencing orgasms as they do for men and that women usually regret engaging in hookups. Both of these beliefs were refuted by the findings of this research. College women reported higher sexual satisfaction when they were romantically and sexually attracted to their hookup partners and when they orgasmed during hookups. Divergent from popular belief, college women reported greater regret when they refrained from higher-order sexual behaviors like penetrative sex and only stuck to lower-order sexual behaviors like kissing and genital touching.

Surge in male sexual victimization. College campuses have earned a notorious reputation of being hotbeds of sexual assault. More often than not, the perpetrators of sexual assault have been men and the victims have been women. However, there are some studies that have shown that college men also experience sexual assault, albeit less often than college men. The results of this research add to this emerging body of literature as it was found that one in five college men reported being sexually assaulted during their last hookup. These incidences of sexual assault included non-consensual sexual touch, being coerced into having sex, or reluctantly performing oral sex on partners. In over 50% of these cases, the sexual perpetrators were college women. College men who met their hookup partners through school were at the highest risk of experiencing sexual assault during hookups compared to any other meeting context.

Although this research contradicted and challenged some popularly held beliefs about the college hookup culture, it also confirmed a number of them. For instance, results showed the continuing dominance of Greek life on the hookup culture as students belonging to fraternities and sororities reported having more hookup partners compared to students who did not belong to these groups. Although college women had as many hookup partners as college men, they discussed the type of physical contact they engaged in during hookups in more abstract terms compared to college men. This could be regarded as their way of saving their reputation lest it gets maligned because of society's double standard that punishes women for their sexual agency but praises men for theirs. Lastly, the result showed that alcohol consumption significantly increased the odds of college women being sexually assaulted during hookups; it had no such effect on college men.

Together with assessing the impact of different meeting contexts on hookups and the shifting gender dynamics in hookups, I also examined the effect of novel practices like sugar dating on students' hookup behaviors. Online sugar dating services such as *Seeking* and *What's Your Price* have made it possible for students to engage in *sugaring*, that is, having casual sexual relationships with older adults in exchange for monetary benefits. Results from my research showed that a small percentage of students engaged in sugaring, but that did not seem to affect their general hookup behaviors.

Finally, I demonstrated the importance of including international students into the larger conversation surrounding hookup culture in American college campuses. According to the findings, international students tended to hook up with other international students compared to Americans, and participating or abstaining from hooking up did not seem to affect their overall sense of belonging. Results also showed that international students engaged in hookups even before attending college in the United States. This indicates that hooking-up is becoming a popular coupling strategy among college-aged students across the world and that hookup culture may no longer be an exclusively American phenomenon.

Overall, I hope that the findings shared in this book have impressed upon readers the necessity of recalibrating our assumptions of the college hookup culture, and in turn, helped them gain an accurate understanding of the current hookup culture in American college campuses.

LIMITATIONS AND FUTURE DIRECTIONS

This research can be improved and expanded in a number of ways. Even though the participants of this research were recruited from a nationally representative sample, the sample was primarily heterosexual, White, Christian. Because of this, the experiences of students who belonged to sexual, racial, and religious minority groups could not be thoroughly accounted for. Also, certain statistical comparisons (for instance, comparing international students with US-born students) could not be performed owing to the limited sample size. Future studies can recruit a larger sample of students and investigate the questions raised in this research to fill these gaps in the existing literature.

Given the nature of the research, students were asked to self-report on matters that were highly sensitive in nature, such as details about their sexual experience, level of intoxication, contraceptive use, and sexual assault. It is possible that students may have provided socially acceptable responses to these survey questions despite the assurance that their identities would be anonymized. Furthermore, since this was an online survey–based research, students could only describe their hookup experiences in limited words. Researchers may consider interviewing students following the survey where students get to expand on their survey responses to provide a more nuanced understanding of their hookup experiences.

Bibliography

Adefuye, A. S., Abiona, T. C., Balogun, J. A., & Lukobo-Durrell, M. (2009). HIV sexual risk behaviors and perception of risk among college students: Implications for planning interventions. *BMC Public Health, 9*(1), 1–13.

Adkins, T., England, P., Risman, B. J., & Ford, J. (2015). Student bodies: Does the sex ratio matter for hooking up and having sex at college? *Social Currents, 2*(2), 144–162.

Al-Shawaf, L., Lewis, D. M., & Buss, D. M. (2015). Disgust and mating strategy. *Evolution and Human Behavior, 36*(3), 199–205.

Al-Tayyib, A. A., McFarlane, M., Kachur, R., & Rietmeijer, C. A. (2009). Finding sex partners on the internet: What is the risk for sexually transmitted infections? *Sexually Transmitted Infections, 85*(3), 216–220.

Allison, R. (2016). Gendered jocks or equal players? Athletic affiliation and hooking up among college students. *Sociological Spectrum, 36*(4), 255–270.

Allport, F. H. (1924). *Social psychology.* Boston: Houghton Mifflin.

Allport, F. H. (1933). *Institutional behavior.* Chapel Hill: University of North Carolina Press.

Andrade, M. S. (2006). International students in English-speaking universities: Adjustment factors. *Journal of Research in International Education, 5*(2), 131–154.

Ansari, A. (2015). *Modern Romance.* London, UK: Allen Lane.

Arnett, J. J. (2004). *Emerging adulthood: The winding road from the late teens through the twenties.* New York: Oxford University Press.

Barnett, M. D., Maciel, I. V., Van Vleet, S., & Marsden III, A. D. (2019). Motivations for faking orgasm and orgasm consistency among young adult women. *Personality and Individual Differences, 149*, 83–87.

Barrios, R. J., & Lundquist, J. H. (2012). Boys just want to have fun? Masculinity, sexual behaviors, and romantic intentions of gay and straight males in college. *Journal of LGBT Youth, 9*(4), 271–296.

BBC.com (2016, February 6). Rise in first-date rape claims linked to online dating. Retrieved from https://www.bbc.com/news/uk-35513052.

Berkowitz, A. (1992). College men as perpetrators of acquaintance rape and sexual assault: A review of recent research. *Journal of American College Health, 40*(4), 175–181.

Berry, J. (1997). Constructing and expanding a framework: Opportunities for developing acculturation research. *Applied Psychology: An International Review, 46*(1), 62–68.

Black, M., Basile, K., Breiding, M., Smith, S., Walters, M., Merrick, M., ... & Stevens, M. (2011). *National intimate partner and sexual violence survey: 2010 summary report*. Retrieved from https://www.cdc.gov/violenceprevention/pdf/nisvs_report2010-a.pdf.

Blow, C. (2008). *The demise of dating*. Retrieved from https://www.nytimes.com/2008/12/13/opinion/13blow.html.

Bogle, K. A. (2008). *Hooking up: Sex, dating, and relationships on campus*. New York: NYU Press.

Bonistall Postel, E. J. (2020). Violence against international students: A critical gap in the literature. *Trauma, Violence, & Abuse, 21*(1), 71–82.

Bower, G. H., Black, J. B., & Turner, T. J. (1979). Scripts in memory for text. *Cognitive Psychology, 11*(2), 177–220.

Bretzman, O. (2019). *The death of dating: Hook-up culture is a relational crisis*. Retrieved from https://www.thecowl.com/opinion/deathofdating.

Brimeyer, T. M., & Smith, W. L. (2012). Religion, race, social class, and gender differences in dating and hooking up among college students. *Sociological Spectrum, 32*(5), 462–473.

Brookstein-Burke, T. (2020). *Tinder: More than a hookup app?* Retrieved from http://udreview.com/tinder-more-than-a-hookup-app/.

Bull, S., & McFarlane, M. (2000). Soliciting sex on the Internet: What are the risks for sexually transmitted diseases and HIV? *Sexually Transmitted Disease, 27*(9), 545–550.

Burdette, A. M., Ellison, C. G., Hill, T. D., & Glenn, N. D. (2009). "Hooking up" at college: Does religion make a difference? *Journal for the Scientific Study of Religion, 48*(3), 535–551.

Burgess, E. W., Locke, H. J., & Thomes, M. M. (1963). *The family: From institution to companionship* (3rd ed.). New York: American Book company.

Burgess, G. H. (2007). Assessment of rape-supportive attitudes and beliefs in college men: Development, reliability, and validity of the rape attitudes and beliefs scale. *Journal of Interpersonal Violence, 22*(8), 973–993.

Buss, D. M., & Schmitt, D. P. (1993). Sexual strategies theory: An evolutionary perspective on human mating. *Psychological Review, 100*(2), 204–32.

Campus Pride Index (2021). https://www.campusprideindex.org/.

Caspi, A., & Gorsky, P. (2006). Online deception: Prevalence, motivation, and emotion. *Cyberpsychology & Behavior, 9*(1), 54–59.

Centers for Disease Control and Prevention (CDC) (2018). Sexually transmitted diseases, adolescents and young adults. https://www.cdc.gov/std/life-stages-populations/adolescents-youngadults.htm.

Chaudhari, P. (2016). *Understanding mixed race and multiethnic students' sense of belonging in college* (Doctoral dissertation, University of Pittsburgh, Pittsburgh, PA, USA). http://dscholarship.pitt.edu/27633/.

Chen, N. (2014). Hooked on Race: An Investigation of the Racialized Hookup Experiences of White, Asian, and Black College Women (Doctoral dissertation, University of Michigan, Michigan, USA). Retrieved from https://deepblue.lib .umich.edu/bitstream/handle/2027.42/107706/nychen.pdf.

Chou, J. (2017). *I'm a sugar baby—& I expect a gift on every first date.* Retrieved from https://www.refinery29.com/en-us/sugar-baby-gifts-first-date-experience.

Christensen, M. A. (2021). "Tindersluts" and "Tinderellas": Examining the digital affordances shaping the (hetero) sexual scripts of young Womxn on Tinder. *Sociological Perspectives, 64*(3), 432–449.

Claxton, S. E., & Van Dulmen, M. H. (2013). Casual sexual relationships and experiences in emerging adulthood. *Emerging Adulthood, 1*(2), 138–150.

Cooper, E. B., Fenigstein, A., & Fauber, R. L. (2014). The faking orgasm scale for women: Psychometric properties. *Archives of Sexual Behavior, 43*(3), 423–435.

Crook, J. (2015). *Hate it or love it, tinder's right swipe limit is working.* Retrieved from https://techcrunch.com/2015/03/12/hate-it-or-love-it-tinders-right-swipe -limit-is-working/.

Currier, D. M. (2013). Strategic ambiguity: Protecting emphasized femininity and hegemonic masculinity in the hookup culture. *Gender & Society, 27*(5), 704–727.

Daly, S. E. (2017). *Sugar babies and sugar daddies: An exploration of sugar dating on Canadian campuses* (Doctoral dissertation, Carleton University, Ottawa, Canada).

Dodge, T., & Jaccard, J. (2002). Participation in athletics and female sexual risk behavior: The evaluation of four causal structures. *Journal of Adolescent Research, 17*(1), 42–67.

Downing-Matibag, T. M., & Geisinger, B. (2009). Hooking up and sexual risk taking among college students: A health belief model perspective. *Qualitative Health Research, 19*(9), 1196–1209.

Eaton, A. A., & Rose, S. (2011). Has dating become more egalitarian? A 35-year review using Sex Roles. *Sex Roles, 64*(11-12), 843–862.

Eaton, A. A., & Rose, S. M. (2012). Scripts for actual first date and hanging-out encounters among young heterosexual Hispanic adults. *Sex Roles, 67*(5), 285–299.

Eaton, A. A., Rose, S. M., Interligi, C., Fernandez, K., & McHugh, M. (2016). Gender and ethnicity in dating, hanging out, and hooking up: Sexual scripts among Hispanic and White young adults. *The Journal of Sex Research, 53*(7), 788–804.

Eisenberg, M. (2001). Differences in sexual risk behaviors between college students with same-sex and opposite-sex experience: Results from a national survey. *Archives of Sexual Behavior, 30*(6), 575–589.

Ellison, N., Heino, R., & Gibbs, J. (2008). Managing impressions online: Self-presentation processes in the online dating environment. *Journal of Computer-Mediated Communication, 11*(2), 415–441.

England, P., & Bearak, J. (2014). The sexual double standard and gender differences in attitudes toward casual sex among US university students. *Demographic Research, 30*, 1327–1338.

England, P., Shafer, E. F., & Fogarty, A. C. K. (2008). Hooking up and forming romantic relationships on today's college campuses. In Michael Kimmel and Amy Aronson (Eds.), *The gendered society reader* (3rd ed., pp. 531–546). New York: Oxford University Press.

England, P., & Thomas, R. J. (2006). The decline of the date and the rise of the college hook up. In A. S. Skolnick & J. S. Skolnick (Eds.), *Family in Transition* (14th ed., pp. 151–162). Boston, MA: Allyn and Bacon.

Fielder, R. L., & Carey, M. P. (2010). Prevalence and characteristics of sexual hookups among first-semester female college students. *Journal of Sex & Marital Therapy*, *36*(4), 346–359.

Fishbein, M., & Ajzen, I. (1975). *Belief, attitude, intention and behavior*. Boston, MA: Addison-Wesley.

Fisher, B. S., Daigle, L. E., & Cullen, F. T. (2010). What distinguishes single from recurrent sexual victims? The role of lifestyle routine activities and first incident characteristics. *Justice Quarterly*, *27*(1), 102–129.

Flack Jr, W. F., Hansen, B. E., Hopper, A. B., Bryant, L. A., Lang, K. W., Massa, A. A., & Whalen, J. E. (2016). Some types of hookups may be riskier than others for campus sexual assault. *Psychological Trauma: Theory, Research, Practice, and Policy*, *8*(4), 413–420.

Ford, J., & Soto-Marquez, J. G. (2016). Sexual assault victimization among straight, gay/lesbian, and bisexual college students. *Violence and Gender*, *3*(2), 107–115.

Forsman, R. L. (2017). Prevalence of sexual assault victimization among college men, aged 18–24: A review. *Journal of Evidence-Informed Social Work*, *14*(6), 421–432.

Fox, J., & Vendemia, M. A. (2016). Selective self-presentation and social comparison through photographs on social networking sites. *Cyberpsychology, Behavior, and Social Networking*, *19*(10), 593–600.

Frederick, D. A., John, H. K. S., Garcia, J. R., & Lloyd, E. A. (2018). Differences in orgasm frequency among gay, lesbian, bisexual, and heterosexual men and women in a US national sample. *Archives of Sexual Behavior*, *47*(1), 273–288.

Friedman, M. S., Marshal, M. P., Guadamuz, T. E., Wei, C., Wong, C. F., Saewyc, E. M., & Stall, R. (2011). A meta-analysis of disparities in childhood sexual abuse, parental physical abuse, and peer victimization among sexual minority and sexual nonminority individuals. *American Journal of Public Health*, *101*(8), 1481–1494.

Garcia, J. R., & Reiber, C. (2008). Hook-up behavior: A biopsychosocial perspective. *Journal of Social, Evolutionary, and Cultural Psychology*, *2*(4), 192–208.

Garcia, J. R., Reiber, C., Massey, S. G., & Merriwether, A. M. (2012). Sexual hookup culture: A review. *Review of General Psychology*, *16*(2), 161–176.

Gareis, E. (2012). Intercultural friendship: Effects of home and host region. *Journal of International and Intercultural Communication*, *5*(4), 309–328.

Garneau, C., Olmstead, S. B., Pasley, K., & Fincham, F. D. (2013). The role of family structure and attachment in college student hookups. *Archives of Sexual Behavior*, *42*(8), 1473–1486.

Glickman, A. R., & La Greca, A. M. (2004). The dating anxiety scale for adolescents: Scale development and associations with adolescent functioning. *Journal of Clinical Child and Adolescent Psychology*, *33*(3), 566–578.

Gorer, G (1964). *The American People: A study in national character.* New York: Norton.

Grantsolutions.gov (2018). *FY18 Announcement of Availability of Funds for Phase I Replicating Programs (Tier 1) Effective in the Promotion of Healthy Adolescence and the Reduction of Teenage Pregnancy and Associated Risk Behaviors.* https://www.grantsolutions.gov/gs/preaward/previewPublicAnnouncement.do?id =61741.

Griffin, M., Canevello, A., & McAnulty, R. D. (2018). Motives and concerns associated with geosocial networking app usage: An exploratory study among heterosexual college students in the United States. *Cyberpsychology, Behavior, and Social Networking, 21*(4), 268–275.

Grello, C. M., Welsh, D. P., & Harper, M. S. (2006). No strings attached: The nature of casual sex in college students. *Journal of Sex Research, 43*(3), 255–267.

Guadagno, R. E., Okdie, B. M., & Kruse, S. A. (2012). Dating deception: Gender, online dating, and exaggerated self-presentation. *Computers in Human Behavior, 28*(2), 642–647.

Hall, W. J., Erausquin, J. T., Nichols, T. R., Tanner, A. E., & Brown-Jeffy, S. (2018). Relationship intentions, race, and gender: Student differences in condom use during hookups involving vaginal sex. *Journal of American College Health, 67*(8), 733–742.

Heldman, C., & Wade, L. (2010). Hook-up culture: Setting a new research agenda. *Sexuality Research and Social Policy, 7*(4), 323–333.

Helm, H. W., Jr., Gondra, S. D., & McBride, D. C. (2015). Hook-up culture among college students: A comparison of attitudes toward hooking-up based on ethnicity and gender. *North American Journal of Psychology, 17*(2), 221–231.

Hendrick, C., Hendrick, S. S., & Reich, D. A. (2006). The brief sexual attitudes scale. *Journal of Sex Research, 43*(1), 76–86.

Herbenick, D., Eastman-Mueller, H., Fu, T. C., Dodge, B., Ponander, K., & Sanders, S. A. (2019). Women's sexual satisfaction, communication, and reasons for (No longer) faking orgasm: findings from a US Probability sample. *Archives of Sexual Behavior, 48*(8), 2461–2472.

Herman, R. D. (1955). The "going steady" complex: A re-examination. *Marriage and Family Living, 17*(1), 36–40.

Hines, D. A., Armstrong, J. L., Reed, K. P., & Cameron, A. Y. (2012). Gender differences in sexual assault victimization among college students. *Violence and Victims, 27*(6), 922–940.

Hsieh, C. (2018). *3 guys on what it's really like to be a sugar baby.* Retrieved from https://www.cosmopolitan.com/sex-love/a15898507/male-sugar-baby/.

Hwang, E., Martirosyan, N. M., & Moore, G. W. (2016). A review of literature on adjustment issues of international students: Recommendations for future practices and research. *Global Perspectives and Local Challenges Surrounding International Student Mobility*, 223–242.

Icefmonitor.org (2019). *US colleges continue to strengthen links with education agents.* https://monitor.icef.com/2019/07/us-colleges-continue-to-strengthen-links -with-education-agents/.

Iie.org (2019). *Number of International Students in the United States hits all-time high.* https://www.iie.org/Why-IIE/Announcements/2019/11/Number-of -International-Students-in-the-United-States-Hits-All-Time-High.

Jablin, F. M. (2000). Organizational entry, assimilation, and disengagement/exit. In F. M.Jablin & L. L. Putman (Eds.), *The New Handbook of Organizational Communication* (pp. 732–818). Thousand Oaks, CA: Sage.

Julian, K. (2018). Why are young people having so little sex? Retrieved from https:// www.theatlantic.com/magazine/archive/2018/12/the-sex-recession/573949/.

Johnson, B. K., & Ranzini, G. (2018). Click here to look clever: Self-presentation via selective sharing of music and film on social media. *Computers in Human Behavior, 82,* 148–158.

Katz, J., & Schneider, M. E. (2013). Casual hook up sex during the first year of college: Prospective associations with attitudes about sex and love relationships. *Archives of Sexual Behavior, 42*(8), 1451–1462.

Kim, Y. K., Collins, C. S., Rennick, L. A., & Edens, D. (2017). College experiences and outcomes among international undergraduate students at research universities in the United States: A comparison to their domestic peers. *Journal of International Students, 7*(2), 395–420.

Kingree, J. B., Braithwaite, R., & Woodring, T. (2000). Unprotected sex as a function of alcohol and marijuana use among adolescent detainees. *Journal of Adolescent Health, 27*(3), 179–185.

Kitchener, C. (2014). *How sugar daddies are financing college education.* Retrieved from https://www.theatlantic.com/education/archive/2014/09/how-sugar-daddies -are-financing-college-education/379533/.

Krebs, C. P., Lindquist, C. H., Warner, T. D., Fisher, B. S., & Martin, S. L. (2009). The differential risk factors of physically forced and alcohol-or other drug-enabled sexual assault among university women. *Violence and Victims, 24*(3), 302–321.

Kuperberg, A., & Padgett, J. E. (2015). Dating and hooking up in college: Meeting contexts, sex, and variation by gender, partner's gender, and class standing. *Journal of Sex Research, 52*(5), 517–531.

Kuperberg, A., & Padgett, J. E. (2016). The role of culture in explaining college students' selection into hookups, dates, and long-term romantic relationships. *Journal of Social and Personal Relationships, 33*(8), 1070–1096.

Kuperberg, A., & Padgett, J. E. (2017). Partner meeting contexts and risky behavior in college students' other-sex and same-sex hookups. *The Journal of Sex Research, 54*(1), 55–72.

LaBrie, J. W., Hummer, J. F., Ghaidarov, T. M., Lac, A., & Kenney, S. R. (2014). Hooking up in the college context: The event-level effects of alcohol use and partner familiarity on hookup behaviors and contentment. *Journal of Sex Research, 51*(1), 62–73.

Lambert, T. A., Kahn, A. S., & Apple, K. J. (2003). Pluralistic ignorance and hooking up. *Journal of Sex Research, 40*(2), 129–133.

Lebowitz, S. (2017). *'Sugar babies' get gifts and cash from their 'sugar daddies' -- but some also get business advice, mentorship, and investments.* Retrieved from

https://www.businessinsider.com.au/seeking-arrangement-sugar-dating-investors
-mentors-2018-6.

Lee-Won, R. J., Shim, M., Joo, Y. K., & Park, S. G. (2014). Who puts the best "face" forward on Facebook?: Positive self-presentation in online social networking and the role of self-consciousness, actual-to-total Friends ratio, and culture. *Computers in Human Behavior, 39*, 413–423.

LeFebvre, L. E. (2018). Swiping me off my feet: Explicating relationship initiation on Tinder. *Journal of Social and Personal Relationships, 35*(9), 1205–1229.

Lenze, T. A. (2020). *Student sugar dating: Sugar babies' perceptions of their decisions to begin, continue, or desist* (Doctoral dissertation, Bowling Green State University, Ohio, USA).

Lewis, M. A., Granato, H., Blayney, J. A., Lostutter, T. W., & Kilmer, J. R. (2012). Predictors of hooking up sexual behaviors and emotional reactions among US college students. *Archives of Sexual Behavior, 41*(5), 1219–1229.

Littleton, H., Downs, E., & Rudolph, K. (2020). The sexual victimization experiences of men attending college: A mixed methods investigation. *Sex Roles, 83*(9), 595–608.

Lowrie, S. H. (1951). Dating theories and student responses. *American Sociological Review, 16*(3), 334–340.

Luo, J., & Jamieson-Drake, D. (2013). Examining the educational benefits of interacting with international students. *Journal of International Students, 3*(2), 85–101.

Mahay, J., & Laumann, E. O. (2004). Meeting and mating over the life course. In E. O. Laumann, S. Ellingson, J. Mahay, A. Paik & Y. Youm (Eds.), *The sexual organization of the city* (pp. 127–164). Chicago, IL: University of Chicago Press.

Mays, V. M., & Cochran, S. D. (2001). Mental health correlates of perceived discrimination among lesbian, gay, and bisexual adults in the United States. *American Journal of Public and Social Psychology, 97*(1), 103–122.

McClintock, E. A. (2010). When does race matter? Race, sex, and dating at an elite university. *Journal of Marriage and Family, 72*(1), 45–72.

McCoy, M. G., Welling, L. L., & Shackelford, T. K. (2015). Development and initial psychometric assessment of the reasons for pretending orgasm inventory. *Evolutionary Psychology, 13*(1), 129–139.

Mellins, C. A., Walsh, K., Sarvet, A. L., Wall, M., Gilbert, L., Santelli, J. S., ... & Hirsch, J. S. (2017). Sexual assault incidents among college undergraduates: Prevalence and factors associated with risk. *PLoS one, 12*(11), e0186471.

Milhausen, R. R., & Herold, E. S. (1999). Does the sexual double standard still exist? Perceptions of university women. *Journal of Sex Research, 36*(4), 361–368.

Miller, A. (2011). Sugar dating: A new take on an old issue. *Buffalo Journal of Gender, Law & Social Policy, 20*, 33–68.

Monto, M., & Milrod, C. (2020). Perceptions of provider power among sex buyers. *Sexualities, 23*(4), 630–644.

Mosley, I. (2009, April). *Promiscuity and GPA: Does hooking up interfere with higher education?* Paper presented at the Undergraduate Research and Scholarship Conference, Boise State University, Idaho, USA.

Motyl, J. (2013). Trading sex for college tuition: How sugar daddy "dating" sites may be sugar coating prostitution. *Penn State Law Review, 117*(3), 927–957.

Murnen, S. K., & Kohlman, M. H. (2007). Athletic participation, fraternity membership, and sexual aggression among college men: A meta-analytic review. *Sex Roles, 57*(1–2), 145–157.

New Citi/Seventeen Survey (2013). *College students take control of their financial futures.* Retrieved from https://www.citigroup.com/citi/news/2013/130807a.htm.

New York University (2011). *2005–2011 online college social life survey.* Retrieved from https://pages.nyu.edu/ocsls/2010/codebook/first.met.at.html.

Nicolson, P., & Burr, J. (2003). What is 'normal' about women's (hetero) sexual desire and orgasm?: A report of an in-depth interview study. *Social Science & Medicine, 57*(9), 1735–1745.

O'Keeffe, P. (2013). A Sense of belonging: Improving student retention. *College Student Journal, 47* (4), 605–613.

Olmstead, S. B., Billen, R. M., Conrad, K. A., Pasley, K., & Fincham, F. D. (2013). Sex, commitment, and casual sex relationships among college men: A mixed-methods analysis. *Archives of Sexual Behavior, 42*(4), 561–571.

Olmstead, S. B., Conrad, K. A., & Anders, K. M. (2018). First semester college students' definitions of and expectations for engaging in hookups. *Journal of Adolescent Research, 33*(3), 275–305.

Opendoorsdata.org (2019). *All places of origin of international scholars.* https://opendoorsdata.org/data/international-scholars/all-places-of-origin/.

Owen, J., & Fincham, F. D. (2011). Young adults' emotional reactions after hooking up encounters. *Archives of Sexual Behavior, 40*(2), 321–330.

Owen, J., Fincham, F. D., & Moore, J. (2011). Short-term prospective study of hooking up among college students. *Archives of Sexual Behavior, 40*(2), 331–341.

Owen, J. J., Rhoades, G. K., Stanley, S. M., & Fincham, F. D. (2010). "Hooking up" among college students: Demographic and psychosocial correlates. *Archives of Sexual Behavior, 39*(3), 653–663.

Paul, E. L., & Hayes, K. A. (2002). The casualties of casual sex: A qualitative exploration of the phenomenology of college students' hookups. *Journal of Social and Personal Relationships, 19*(5), 639–661.

Paul, E. L., McManus, B., & Hayes, A. (2000). "Hookups": Characteristics and correlates of college students' spontaneous and anonymous sexual experiences. *Journal of Sex Research, 37*(1), 76–88.

Peter, J., & Valkenburg, P. M. (2007). Who looks for casual dates on the internet? A test of the compensation and the recreation hypotheses. *New Media & Society, 9*(3), 455–474.

Pham, J. M. (2017). Beyond hookup culture: Current trends in the study of college student sex and where to next. *Sociology Compass, 11*(8), e12499.

Piemonte, J. L., Conley, T. D., & Gusakova, S. (2019). Orgasm, gender, and responses to heterosexual casual sex. *Personality and Individual Differences, 151*, 109487.

Postell, B. E. J. (2015). *International graduate students' risk and vulnerability to sexual violence and victimization* (Doctoral dissertation, University of Delaware, Delaware, USA). http://udspace.udel.edu/handle/19716/.

Ray, R., & Rosow, J. A. (2010). Getting off and getting intimate: How normative institutional arrangements structure black and white fraternity men's approaches toward women. *Men and Masculinities, 12*(5), 523–546.

Regnerus, M. D. (2007). *Forbidden fruit: Sex and religion in the lives of American teenagers.* New York: Oxford University Press.

Reiber, C., & Garcia, J. R. (2010). Hooking up: Gender differences, evolution, and pluralistic ignorance. *Evolutionary Psychology, 8*(3), 390–404.

Reiss, I. L. (1956). The double standard in premarital sexual intercourse: A neglected concept. *Social Forces, 34,* 224–230.

Rose, S., & Frieze, I. H. (1989). Young singles' scripts for a first date. *Gender & Society, 3,* 258–268.

Rosenfeld, M. J., & Thomas, R. J. (2012). Searching for a mate: The rise of the Internet as a social intermediary. *American Sociological Review, 77*(4), 523–547.

Rosenfeld, M. J., Thomas, R. J., & Hausen, S. (2019). Disintermediating your friends: How online dating in the United States displaces other ways of meeting. *Proceedings of the National Academy of Sciences, 116*(36), 17753–17758.

Rusu, O. (2019). *Beyond $300 billion: The global impact of International Students.* https://studyportals.com/intelligence/global-impact-of-international-students/.

Sales, J. (2015). *Tinder and the dawn of the "dating apocalypse"* Retrieved from https://www.vanityfair.com/culture/2015/08/tinder-hook-up-culture-end-of-dating

Scull, M. T. (2020). "It's its own thing": A typology of interpersonal sugar relationship scripts. *Sociological Perspectives, 63*(1), 135–158.

Seeking.com (2014, February 13). *Seeking arrangement appears on the view with Jenny McCarthy.* Youtube. https://www.youtube.com/watch?v=py9sLqP2PA8&t=183s.

Seeking.com (2021). *SBU students in the USA.* Retrieved from https://www.seeking.com/p/sugar-baby-university-2021/usa/.

Séguin, L. J., & Milhausen, R. R. (2016). Not all fakes are created equal: Examining the relationships between men's motives for pretending orgasm and levels of sexual desire, and relationship and sexual satisfaction. *Sexual and Relationship Therapy, 31*(2), 159–175.

Sevi, B. (2019). Brief report: Tinder users are risk takers and have low sexual disgust sensitivity. *Evolutionary Psychological Science, 5*(1), 104–108.

Simon, W., & Gagnon, J. H. (2003). Sexual scripts: Origins, influences and changes. *Qualitative Sociology, 26*(4), 491–497.

Smith, A. (2016). *15% of American adults have used online dating sites or mobile dating apps.* Retrieved from https://www.pewresearch.org/internet/2016/02/11/15-percent-of-american-adults-have-used-online-dating-sites-or-mobile-dating-apps/.

Snapp, S., Ryu, E., & Kerr, J. (2015). The upside to hooking up: College students' positive hookup experiences. *International Journal of Sexual Health, 27*(1), 43–56.

Song, J., & Morash, M. (2016). Materialistic desires or childhood adversities as explanations for girls' trading sex for benefits. *International Journal of Offender Therapy and Comparative Criminology, 60*(1), 62–81.

Spell, S. A. (2017). Not just black and white: How race/ethnicity and gender intersect in hookup culture. *Sociology of Race and Ethnicity, 3*(2), 172–187.

Steele, C. M., & Josephs, R. A. (1990). Alcohol myopia: Its prized and dangerous effects. *American Psychologist, 45*(8), 921–933.

Stepp, L. S. (2007). *Unhooked: How young women pursue sex, delay love and lose at both.* New York: Riverhead Books.

Stewart, M. A., Ryan, E. B., & Giles, H. (1985). Accent and social class effects on status and solidarity evaluations. *Personality and Social Psychology Bulletin, 11*(1), 98–105.

Strayhorn, T. L. (2018). *College students' sense of belonging: A key to educational success for all students.* New York: Routledge.

Sumter, S. R., & Vandenbosch, L. (2019). Dating gone mobile: Demographic and personality-based correlates of using smartphone-based dating applications among emerging adults. *New Media & Society, 21*(3), 655–673.

Sumter, S. R., Vandenbosch, L., & Ligtenberg, L. (2017). Love me Tinder: Untangling emerging adults' motivations for using the dating application Tinder. *Telematics and Informatics, 34*(1), 67–78.

Tewksbury, R., & Mustaine, E. E. (2001). Lifestyle factors associated with the sexual assault of men: A routine activity theory analysis. *The Journal of Men's Studies, 9*(2), 153–182.

Thomson Ross, L., Zeigler, S., Kolak, A. M., & Epstein, D. (2015). Sexual hookups and alcohol consumption among African American and Caucasian college students: A pilot study. *The Journal of Psychology, 149*(6), 582–600.

Timmermans, E., & Van den Bulck, J. (2018). Casual sexual scripts on the screen: A quantitative content analysis. *Archives of Sexual Behavior, 47*(5), 1481–1496.

Tomkins, S. S. (1987). Script theory. In J. Aronoff & A. I. Rubin (Eds.), *The emergence of personality* (pp. 147–216). New York: Springer.

Tong, S. T., Hancock, J. T., & Slatcher, R. B. (2016). The influence of technology on romantic relationships: Understanding online dating. In G.Meiselwitz (Ed.), *Social Computing and Social Media* (pp. 162–173). New York, NY: Springer.

Torbenson, C. L (2009). *From the beginning: A history of college fraternities and sororities.* In C. Madison, L. Torbenson, & G. S. Parks (Eds.), *Brothers and sisters: Diversity in college fraternities and sororities* (pp. 15–45). Cranbury, New Jersey: Fairleigh Dickinson University Press.

Townsend, J. M., & Wasserman, T. H. (2011). Sexual hookups amoncollege students: Sex differences in emotional reactions. *Archives of Sexual Behavior, 40*(6), 1173–1181.

Turchik, J. A. (2012). Sexual victimization among male college students: Assault severity, sexual functioning, and health risk behaviors. *Psychology of Men & Masculinity, 13*(3), 243.

Turkle, S. (1995). *Life on the screen: Identity in the age of the Internet.* London: Phoenix.

Twenge, J. M., Sherman, R. A., & Wells, B. E. (2015). Changes in American adults' sexual behavior and attitudes, 1972–2012. *Archives of Sexual Behavior, 44*(8), 2273–2285.

Tybur, J. M., Lieberman, D., & Griskevicius, V. (2009). Microbes, mating, and morality: Individual differences in three functional domains of disgust. *Journal of Personality 97*(1), 103.

Urban, E. L., & Palmer, L. B. (2014). International students as a resource for internationalization of higher education. *Journal of Studies in International Education, 18*(4), 305–324.

Valkenburg, P. M., & Peter, J. (2007). Who visits online dating sites? Exploring some characteristics of online dater. *Cyberpsychology & Behavior, 10,* 849–852.

Wade, L. (2017). *American hookup: The new culture of sex on campus.* New York: W. W. Norton & Company.

Waller, W. (1937). The rating and dating complex. *American Sociological Review, 2*(5), 727–734.

Walsh, J. L., Fielder, R. L., Carey, K. B., & Carey, M. P. (2014). Do alcohol and marijuana use decrease the probability of condom use for college women? *The Journal of Sex Research, 51*(2), 145–158.

Walther, J. B. (1996). Computer-mediated communication: Impersonal, interpersonal, and hyperpersonal interaction. *Communication Research, 23,* 3–44.

Wang, I., Ahn, J. N., Kim, H. J., & Lin-Siegler, X. (2017). Why do international students avoid communicating with Americans? *Journal of International Students, 7*(3), 555–582.

Wasylkiw, L., & Currie, M. (2012). The Animal House effect: How university-themed comedy films affect students' attitudes. *Social Psychology of Education, 15*(1), 25–40.

Watson, R. J., Snapp, S., & Wang, S. (2017). What we know and where we go from here: A review of lesbian, gay, and bisexual youth hookup literature. *Sex Roles, 77*(11), 801–811.

Wells, B. E., & Twenge, J. M. (2005). Changes in young people's sexual behavior and attitudes, 1943–1999: A cross-temporal meta-analysis. *Review of General Psychology, 9*(3), 249–261.

Wexler, S. (2013). *The secret world of sugar babies.* Retrieved from https://www.cosmopolitan.com/lifestyle/advice/a5090/sugar-babies/.

Wiederman, M.W. (2015). Sexual script theory: Past, present, and future. In J. DeLamater & R.F. Plante (Eds.), *Handbook of the Sociology of Sexualities* (pp. 7–22). Switzerland: Springer International Publishing.

Index

About the Author

Aditi Paul, PhD, is professor of communication studies at Pace University in New York City. She uses her multidisciplinary background in computer science and communication to examine the cultural, interpersonal, psychological, and health impact of using communication technologies like social networking sites and online dating services. Aditi's research has been published in top academic journals including *Cyberpsychology, Behavior, and Social Networking* and *Personality and Individual Differences*. Her research has been featured in major media outlets including *The Washington Post, Women's Health, The Telegraph UK, Huffington Post*, and *NBCNews*.

Lucy Dolcich, the coauthor of the chapter "What Happens during a Hookup? Analysis of College Students' Hookup Scripts," is a former student of Aditi Paul at Pace University.